Incarceration Nation

Crossroads in Qualitative Inquiry

Series Editors
Norman K. Denzin, University of Illinois, Urbana-Champaign
Yvonna S. Lincoln, Texas A&M University

ABOUT THE SERIES: Qualitative methods are material and interpretive practices. They do not stand outside politics and cultural criticism. This spirit of critically imagining and pursuing a more democratic society has been a guiding feature of qualitative inquiry from the very beginning. The Crossroads in Qualitative Inquiry series will take up such methodological and moral issues as the local and the global, text and context, voice, writing for the other, and the presence of the author in the text. The Crossroads series understands that the discourses of a critical, moral methodology are basic to any effort to re-engage the promise of the social sciences for democracy in the twenty-first century. This international series creates a space for the exploration of new representational forms and new critical, cultural studies.

SUBMITTING MANUSCRIPTS: Book proposals should be sent to Crossroads in Qualitative Inquiry Series, c/o Norman K. Denzin, Institute for Communication Research, 810 S. Wright Street, University of Illinois, Urbana, Illinois 61801, or emailed to n-denzin@uiuc.edu.

BOOKS IN THIS SERIES:

Incarceration Nation

Investigative Prison Poems of Hope and Terror

STEPHEN JOHN HARTNETT

ALTAMIRA
PRESS

A Division of
ROWMAN & LITTLEFIELD PUBLISHERS, INC.
Walnut Creek • Lanham • New York • Oxford

ALTAMIRA PRESS
A Division of Rowman & Littlefield Publishers, Inc.
1630 North Main Street, #367
Walnut Creek, CA 94596
www.altamirapress.com

Rowman & Littlefield Publishers, Inc.
A Member of the Rowman & Littlefield Publishing Group
4501 Forbes Boulevard, Suite 200
Lanham, MD 20706

PO Box 317
Oxford
OX2 9RU, UK

British Library Cataloguing in Publication Information Available

Library of Congress Cataloging-in-Publication Data

Hartnett, Stephen J.
    Incarceration Nation : investigative prison poems of hope and terror / Stephen John
    Hartnett.
        p. cm.—(Crossroads in qualitative inquiry ; v. 1)
        ISBN: 978-0-7591-0420-4
        1. Prisoners' writings, American—History and criticism. 2. American poetry—20th
    century—History and criticism. 3. Prisoners in literature. 4. Prisons in literature.
    5. Terror in literature. 6. Hope in literature. I. Title. II. Series.

PS153.P74H37 2003
811'.540809206927—dc21

                                                                        2003049550
Printed in the United States of America

♾™ The paper used in this publication meets the minimum requirements of American
National Standard for Information Sciences—Permanence of Paper for Printed Library
Materials, ANSI/NISO Z39.48–1992.

for B.A.K.

ma femme sublime

&

A.H.K.H.

mi cabecita de calabaza

"Hudson River Abstract"

The image on the cover of this book is a reproduction of Anthony Papa's "Hudson River Abstract," a 1992 acrylic painting on canvas board. The image represents Papa's view from his prison cell in New York's Sing Sing Prison, where Papa was sent in 1985 to serve a fifteen-years-to-life mandatory sentence for delivering 4.5 ounces of cocaine. Combining the hope and beauty of painterly abstraction with the harsh reality of living behind a barbed-wire wall, the image resonates with many of the paradoxes addressed in the poems included here.

Prior to his arrest in 1985, Papa owned an auto repair shop in the Bronx and was neither a criminal nor a drug dealer. One evening, a teammate on his Yonkers softball team offered him $500 to deliver a package of cocaine. Papa agreed, only to find that his teammate was an undercover narcotics agent. While in prison, Papa completed a series of highly regarded paintings including "Hudson River Abstract." Recognizing both Papa's artistic talents and the absurdity of sentencing a first-time, nonviolent offender to fifteen-years-to-life for one indiscretion, one tragic lapse in judgement, Governor George Pataki granted Papa clemency on Christmas Eve, 1996. Since his release, Papa has become an activist fighting against the drug war and the prison-industrial-complex. A generous selection of Papa's work may be seen on the Web at www.15yearstolife.com; his *15 to Life: A Casualty of the Drug War* is forthcoming in 2003.

Contents

Foreword

We are honored and pleased to introduce our new series with AltaMira Press with Stephen John Hartnett's powerfully painful, bold, and imaginative new work. *Incarceration Nation: Investigative Prison Poems of Hope and Terror* takes us inside America's prison-industrial-complex, a sprawling network of penal colonies that stretches from coast to coast. Using an innovative writing form that he calls investigative poetry, Hartnett takes us inside this system: we feel it, smell it, and see it, sensing the pain, the sadness, the lost lives warehoused in supermax complexes. Hartnett knows well what he writes about, as this book is the product of twelve years of writing about and protesting at prisons, and nine years of teaching college in Indiana and California prisons. We walk with Stephen and his students past bulletproof doors, down scrubbed white hallways where young men, their heads shaved and hands shackled, shuffle along in humiliation and rage. Relentlessly painful in detail, these poems must be heard as muffled yet loud cries for prison reform and an end to the death penalty. But each poem clings as well to hope, to the belief that inside these prison walls, in their dignified acts of resistance, men dismantle parts of this brutal system, celebrating their own humanity in the process. Hartnett's gift to us—this gift of hope—is to show how acts of resistance can change inhumane systems of social control.

This investigative prison poetry is part of a larger project, anchored in a web of social movements, a decade of prison activism, and the blossoming world of social justice art. Not unlike the antebellum abolitionists in the nineteenth century, today's prison activists also struggle against racism and slavery, crime and punishment under the flag of democracy. Thus offering layered historical observations on our ongoing national struggle for justice, Stephen reminds us that even in its compromised state, democracy is worth fighting for. "We're imperfect people and we don't know what to do, but something must be done. What will our grandchildren say?" This is "Karina's Question," the title of the last poem in this wonderful book, which asks us on every page to renew our commitment to the obligations of engaged and joyous citizenship.

*   *   *   *   *

Our writing practices are never innocent. The technologies of writing and inquiry create gendered texts where desire, intimacy, power, race, ethnicity, and identity come alive. These technologies connect us to qualitative research methods that embody material and interpretive practices. As forms of pedagogy, our methodologies function as educational tools: they help us generate knowledge by exploring ways of seeing, thinking, hearing, speaking, writing, and acting. Our methodologies are therefore always political and performative. We must acknowledge this fact by rooting our methodological and writing performances in a multiracial, equalitarian discourse that strives to honor the best of democracy's promises. This spirit of critically imagining and pursuing a more egalitarian society has always been a guiding feature of qualitative inquiry. As Stephen Hartnett reminds us, radical experiments in democracy have often been accompanied by radical forms of investigation and representation. Walt Whitman, for example, called for a radically democratic poetry, for free-form poems of witness that could embody the great hopes and crushing political contradictions of his slavery-driven democracy. The offerings of a critical, moral methodology are basic to any effort to re-engage the promises of the social sciences for aiding democracy in the twenty-first century as well. Indeed, building on Whitman, Dos Passos, Forché, Conquergood, and others, and including a vast array of imprisoned poets and prison activists, *Incarceration Nation* demonstrates how exploring new representational forms is central to this project of merging methodological inquires and political practices.

Hartnett's *Incarceration Nation: Investigative Prison Poems of Hope and Terror* is an outstanding exemplar of this new form of action inquiry. It is therefore appropriate that it is the inaugural work in this new series, called "Crossroads in Qualitative Inquiry." Our intentions, like Hartnett's, are clear. We want to encourage and produce works that embody critical, reflexive thinking. Such works move outward from the writer's experiences to expose the injustices of class, race, and gender privilege that prevail in specific locations and sites. Such works will question the structures of white patriarchy and global capitalism while helping people imagine realistic utopias, thus fostering hope for a more just social world.

Norman K. Denzin and Yvonna S. Lincoln, Series Editors

Acknowledgments

Writing these acknowledgments has been a humbling experience, for as I have thought about what to say and whom to thank I have realize that there are a remarkable number of people whose kindness I need to repay, whose support I need to acknowledge, and whose work as teachers, students, activists, and artists I want to honor. Indeed, while I take full responsibility for whatever criticism may fall on the poems that follow, I nonetheless think of this work as feeding off of and participating in a web of social movements, many of which address the prison-industrial-complex. In fact, the past decades have witnessed an explosion of prison activism so creative and powerful that I am hard pressed not to make comparisons to the antebellum abolitionists, our nineteenth century forebears who fought against slavery and racism. I find such comparisons simultaneously daunting and empowering, for they demonstrate not only that democracy has always been difficult, and that ancient political prejudices haunt our present struggles, but also that democracy has always been and still is worth fighting for.

The poems included here represent experiences gathered over twelve years of writing about and protesting at prisons, and nine years of teaching college in Indiana and California prisons, where I had the life-changing opportunity of working with students who taught me more than I taught them. From Indiana prisons I want to thank Greg, Julius, D.J., Raz, Cobb, Paddle Foot, Big Will, Sol, Wolfy, Travis, Jalaal, Bones, Kilo, T., Dale, Tinnin-Bey, Buddy Love, Todrei, L.O., Burkhart, E.J., Shaka, and too many other students to mention. From the many wonderful students at San Quentin I want to thank especially Lefty, Swami, Barney, Eddie, Mike, David, Ronnie, Rick, Phillip, Hal, Ronald, Melvyn, Watani, Fajardo, Rhino, Don, D.C., Jason, Tim, Rachman, and Leonard. I fear I can not do justice to the debt I owe these men and their classmates, as their stories, voices, tragedies, and persistent hopes in the face of horror are largely responsible for first forcing and then enabling me to consider the difficulties of democracy. My work with these men was propelled largely by the energy of Jon Rutter, Sean McPhetridge, Jody Lewen, and Steve Guy, each an inspiration in their generous work as prison teachers. My San Quentin experience was made even more joyous by the presence of my U.C. Berkeley students, who volunteered in droves to tutor my San Quentin students. I try to depict the utopian energy of their work in the opening sections of "Love and Death in California," but want to offer thanks here as well to Brian, Cat, Sharon, Shelly, Peter, Shayne, Todd, Steven, Anne, Hong, Rose, David, Rachel, Tara, Ori, Emile, Roberto, Nicole, and Ashley.

Preliminary work on "Karina's Question" was made possible by a four day retreat at The Blue Mountain Arts Center, in upstate New York, in conjunction with the Blue Mountain Artists Against Massive Incarceration, a group convened by Buzz Alexander in the Summer of 1997. In 1998 the group met at the Marin Headlands Center for The Arts, just outside San Francisco, where Karina Epperlein again repeated the question that concludes this book. I met Richard Kamler and Robin Sohnen at this latter gathering and have been working with them ever since on "The Waiting Room," a traveling anti-death penalty art installation for which I host community conversations about crime, punishment, and democracy. While working on "The Waiting Room" and other Blue Mountain actions, Buzz, Richard, and Robin have offered constant inspiration, love, and support.

Along with the ideas and energies shared by my fellow Blue Mountain Artists and the hundreds of participants in "The Waiting Room," I am grateful for the lively exchanges enabled by Critical Resistance, a group of over 2,500 artists, activists, teachers, and students who gathered in the Fall of 1998 in Berkeley and then in the Spring of 2001 in New York City. I am particularly thankful for the work of H. Bruce Franklin, who, both at Critical Resistance and in his published work, has taught us to recognize that prison writing is among the oldest, most vibrant, and most important sub-genres of American Literature. There is much more to be said here regarding the work of those who bring prison poets into the public—thank you Judith, Bell, Katie, Dick, Tory, Raylene, and others—but I will save those words for the Introduction. Nonetheless, I want to say a special thank you to Judith Tannenbaum, both for commenting upon the manuscript and mentoring so many of us in the movement.

Some of these poems have appeared previously (or are forthcoming) in *Broken Chains*, *Dark Night Field Notes*, *Left Curve*, *The Radical Philosophy Review*, *The Future of Performance Studies* (Sheron Dailey, ed.), and *Dignified Deaths, Joyous Wakes: Reflections on Dying and Death in America* (Helen Cooper and E. Ann Kaplan, eds.). I am grateful to these sources both for their permission to reprint material and for their editors' helpful suggestions. Sheron Dailey in particular was an encouraging and empowering voice when I needed it badly. I have performed many of these poems in New York, Oakland, Berkeley, San Francisco, St. Louis, The Blue Mountain Arts Center, and, in earlier drafts, as part of The Voices of the Americas Poetry Series, hosted by Danny Postel and Free Associations Radio at the Tres en Uno Café in Chicago. I am grateful to the organizers of these events, especially to Danny, who has for the past twelve years been one of the heartland's primary engines of radical artistic and political activity, and Larry Frey, who has stood for over a decade as a model engaged scholar.

For access to the archival materials used in "'Do Right and Fear Not!': Five Meditations on San Quentin," I am grateful to the staff of the Bancroft Library at The University of California, Berkeley, and the Marin County Historical Society.

I completed this book in the Fall of 2002, while serving as an Assistant Professor of Speech Communication at the University of Illinois, where I have had the good fortune of receiving help from my remarkable colleagues. Adam Sutcliffe (History) and Joshua Esty (English) both commented upon the Introduction; Brett Kaplan (Comparative Literature) edited the entire manuscript; Zohreh Sullivan (English) has for the past four years prodded me forward with warm ideas and unbelievable cooking; Norm Denzin (Institute of Communications Research) has graciously drawn me into his vibrant world and offered kind advice whenever asked; Joshua Barbour (Speech Communication) edited the manuscript; and my Department Heads, first David Swanson and now Barbara Wilson, have structured my teaching and other responsibilities so as to provide maximum time for writing and activism—thank you all. There are many other friends and colleagues who deserve high praise for their support and guidance, but I have saved my words for them for the Introduction that follows.

Finally, as indicated both on the dedication page and in "Love and Death in California," this book is for my wife, Brett, and my daughter, Anya, who each day teach me new things about love and hope.

Stephen John Hartnett
Champaign, Illinois, December of the year Two-Thousand and Two A.D., and of our National Independence the Two-Hundred and Twenty-Sixth.

Introduction: A Reader's Guide to Investigative Prison Poetry

Love the earth and sun and the animals, despise riches, give alms to every one that asks, stand up for the stupid and crazy, devote your income and labor to others, hate tyrants, argue not concerning God . . . take off your hat to nothing known or unknown or to any man or number of men . . . re-examine all you have been told at school or church or in any book, dismiss whatever insults your soul, and your very flesh shall be a great poem.

Thus Walt Whitman offers some of his typically blustery advice on how to make one's life into a poem. Critics (including myself) have observed for almost one-hundred-and-fifty years that such pronouncements lead rather quickly to a sense of overstuffed grandeur if not downright delusion, yet who can argue with Whitman's remarkable energy and dynamism? Who can begrudge a poet committed to a life so egalitarian, spiritual, aesthetic, and kind? I am no Whitman, that's for sure, but it seems fitting to begin this Introduction by arguing for a return to a vision of America and American poetry more consistent with Whitman's. The investigative prison poems printed here thus seek to enliven that lost Whitmanesque tradition of seeing America as the world's best and most radical experiment in democracy, for even when that experiment is botched in so many ways—as are addressed here in relentlessly painful detail—the vision is still worth fighting for. I argue in these poems that while the prison-industrial-complex poses one of our most serious threats to that vision, the prisoners, teachers, activists, and poets celebrated herein offer perhaps our best hope for recasting it in a fresh multiracial and egalitarian light. Whereas many activists and scholars have made this argument in prose, I pursue it below via poems that are laden with research, hence merging the evidence-gathering force of scholarship with the emotion-producing force of poetry. In so doing, I hope to inhabit the cosmic (and of course slightly crazy) bird's eye view that makes Whitman's poems so maddening, sometimes funny, and often miraculously insightful regarding what is best and worst about America.[1]

Along with this hope of reviving a Whitmanesque sense of a critical yet lovingly political poetry committed to advancing the cause of democracy in America, the investigative prison poems in this book have been written for a number of more immediate personal and political reasons: to honor the activists, prisoners, teachers, and artists I have encountered in twelve years of teaching in, writing about, and protesting at prisons; to sublimate the horror I have absorbed while working in the bowels of the prison-industrial-complex; to investigate the economic, racial, political, cultural, and historical impulses driving our criminal justice system in particular and our culture in general toward barbarism; to experiment with the ways scholarly research and poetry may be combined in a new persuasive genre; and to remember with as vivid detailing as possible and as much supporting research as possible moments that and characters who have taught me lessons large and small about the humbling complexity of holding onto hope in the face of terror. Written both to expose the tragedy of the prison-industrial-complex and to celebrate the energy of those who fight against it, these poems necessarily wobble through utter despair to unfounded hope to dumb confusion, through portrayals of villainous cruelty to uncommon loving to simple kindness—and of course through all the gray areas that dominate the existential complexities of daily life.

It comes as no surprise, then, to know that some readers have found these investigative poems difficult to understand, not so much because of their confounded emotions and sometimes scathing politics, but because they so actively refuse to fit into traditional genres of textual production. Indeed, ever since I first began writing, performing, and then publishing what I call investigative prison poetry, readers have responded in roughly the same ways: some professional poets have tended to find the work not poetic enough and too information-heavy; some scholars have tended to find the work emotionally charged and politically savvy while not understanding the need to convey it in poetic form; some activists have felt that the work's emphasis on the mutual reciprocity of obligations for both oppression and liberation is too self-implicating to be useful for the purposes of political muckraking; and then, thankfully, others of all varieties have found the work exciting, hopeful, and even redemptive. This spread of responses would not be uncommon if not for the fact that it so consistently revolves around questions of genre: are these investigative poems qualitative research, critical ethnography, political manifesto, fractured autobiography, tainted confession, or fictional narrative? "But is it poetry?" has been asked by poets about as often as "But is it scholarship?" has been asked by academics; both questions have been asked about as often as "But can poetry make a difference?" has been asked by activists. While such questions are always welcome challenges to think more carefully about the poems, they also indicate the sad convergence of relentless intellectual specialization, diminished political expectations, and crippling artistic insecurity. It is as if an entire generation of Americans has forgotten Ralph Waldo Emerson's heroic 1844 demand that a poet should strive toward becoming "the Knower, the Doer and the Sayer." Emerson told his readers that Knowing, Doing, and Saying "stand respectively for the love of truth, for the love of good, and for the love of beauty." Although postmodern criticism has made notions of truth, good, and beauty passé, I can think of worse things than trying to live up to Emerson's hopes for a new American art—look what such aspirations did for Whitman![2]

Hoping that I might provide some helpful answers to the questions and problems raised above, which in turn may help readers enjoy the poems that follow more fully, the editors of the new series for which this book is the first volume have asked me to share these opening thoughts regarding not only the *hows* and *whys* of investigative poetry, but of the larger intellectual, political, and poetic traditions that have inspired this work. It seems impossible to begin such an introduction without first noting that arguments over the possible relationships among poetry, politics, and social justice are as old as civilization itself. As Sven Birkerts observes, "The poetry/politics debate began when Plato booted the poet from his ideal Republic, maybe even sooner; it will go on so long as there is language." But unlike Birkerts and the hundreds of other critics who have weighed in with weighty pronouncements on one aspect of this debate, often in tones that one can only describe as partisan at best, shrill at worst, I want to honor the epic and sometimes comic nature of that debate without descending into it. Instead, I offer readers these opening comments in the humble sense of celebrating some veins of work that I have found edifying. My comments here may be taken, then, not so much as levying an argument about how I think poets, activists, and scholars should proceed so much as sharing some hopefully pedagogical thoughts on the activist traditions, literary models, and personal inspirations that have led me to produce these investigative prison poems.[3]

This introduction accordingly unfolds in four movements. First, I review the literature regarding the recent turn across the humanities to a concern with social justice, hence grounding my work within the tradition of engaged scholars who use their positions as teachers and writers to help expand democratic rights, economic opportunities, and cultural aspirations to an ever larger circle of Americans. Second, I offer an enthusiast's road guide to my favorite prison poetry, including works by prisoners and their allies, hence aligning my own work with a long and honorable tradition that sees questions of crime, violence, and punishment as crucial components of our national history. Third, I show how concerns for social justice and a commitment to writing a political poetry of witness have been merged in the exemplary works of John Dos Passos, Carolyn Forché, and Peter Dale Scott, thus celebrating three models for producing texts that are simultaneously historical, political, personal, philosophical, and beautiful. Fourth, as a practical culmination of the first three sections, I offer readers some cursory suggestions on how to approach the poems in this volume. Taken as a whole, the introduction demonstrates the academic, poetic, and activist traditions that energize my own work, hopefully making the poems in this volume feel a little less like intruders from a strange land and more like neighbors who, upon closer scrutiny, seem uncannily familiar. To help us remember that the investigative poems included here are above all else tributes to the struggles of those enmeshed within the prison-industrial-complex, I end each subsection of this Introduction with sections of poems written by prisoners.

*   *   *   *   *

I breathe the wintry morning breeze
soaking in nature's peaceful glory
feeling the strength of solitude
absorbing the blessings the day brings
encompassing my being
offering me peace
in mind and body

I call upon the Mountain God
to give me strength and wisdom
to withstand fear oppression hatred

fading now mercifully
as the morning sunlight
warms my face
we merge within these prison walls
alone in the yard
filled with compassion
wonder and hope[4]

Social Justice & The Obligations and Opportunities of Engaged Scholars

I hope readers approach *Democracy is Difficult* as part of a much larger flood of materials calling upon professional academics to become more active in their communities' various struggles for social justice. While it is not difficult to piece together a loose genealogy of intellectuals concerned over the past centuries with issues of social justice, I am glad to see that in recent years scholars across a variety of disciplines have begun arguing in a systematic manner that those teacher-activists committed to the ends of social justice while still cherishing the wondrously messy means of democratic life need to approach issues of social justice not only as sites of research, but also as sites of engagement with disadvantaged communities. Many of these ideas were first made concrete for me in the work of Dwight Conquergood, a Performance Studies professor at Northwestern University, who spent years doing research on and advocating on behalf of the gangs with whom he lived as a neighbor, teacher, and substitute father figure in the decimated Cabrini Green public housing of Chicago. Conquergood lectured widely about his experiences and wrote about them and their implications for academics and activists in two brilliant articles published in 1994 and 1995. Inspired by Conquergood's bravery, Larry Frey, Barnett Pearce, Mark Pollock, Lee Artz, and Bren Murphy, colleagues at Loyola University, Chicago, implored their fellow Speech Communication scholars in 1996 to conduct research "not only *about* but *for* and *in the interests of* the people with whom" the research is conducted. This means that scholars can no longer assume they are objective outsiders analyzing static objects of inquiry; instead, in this new model of engaged scholarship, researchers become subjects mutually enmeshed in the processes they are studying. Frey and his colleagues thus asked engaged scholars to channel their academic work toward pressing community needs, and thus to produce works that "foreground ethical concerns," "commit to structural analyses of ethical problems," "adopt an activist orientation," and "seek identification with others." I had the good fortune of living in Chicago when Conquergood and Frey published these works, and so was mentored by them to push my scholarship and activism in new directions. Indeed, taking Conquergood and Frey's ideas seriously meant that I could not teach in prisons without in turn becoming both an activist working for prisoners' rights and a historian of America's long obsession with crime and criminals. The investigative prison poems included in this volume thus stand in many regards as my attempt to embody the ideals forwarded by Conquergood and Frey.[5]

For more specific ways to think about the prospects of teaching on, researching about, and fighting for social justice, I have been influenced by Pierre Bourdieu's "For a Scholarship with Commitment," an essay adapted from a presentation he gave as part of a panel organized by Edward Said for the 1999 meeting of the Modern Language Association (MLA). Bourdieu recommends that scholars hoping to make a difference pursue four goals: (1) "produce and disseminate instruments of defense against symbolic domination"; (2) engage in "discursive critique," meaning analyses of the "sociological determinants that bear on the producers of dominant discourse"; (3) "counter the pseudoscientific authority of authorized experts"; and (4) "help to create social conditions for the collective production of realist utopias." We may conceptualize these imperatives as pointing to four modes of critical activity: first, helping to teach and popularize the critical thinking skills necessary for citizens to become more conscientious consumers of mass media—we may think of this as *debunking cultural symbolism*; second, demonstrating through rigorous case studies how dominant discourse reflects the economic imperatives of elites—we may think of this as *analyzing class privilege*; third, revealing and helping others to reveal the political assumptions and biases of experts within specific fields of inquiry—we may think of this as *becoming rhetorical critics*; and fourth, both imagining and advocating for alternative ways of being—we may think of this as *inventing new possibilities*. In that same panel, Elaine Scarry put this fourth imperative in lovely terms—terms that would make Emerson and Whitman proud—arguing that teachers of literature and the arts share a special burden to cultivate in both their students and their communities "a reverence for the work of the imagination." What better way to cultivate this reverence and to address Bourdieu's first three critical imperatives than by writing investigative poetry?[6]

The one obvious shortcoming of the suggestions of Bourdieu, Scarry, and their fellow MLA participants is that even while asking us to pursue scholarship with commitment they tend to privilege certain traditional forms of textual production, hence excluding (perhaps unwittingly, I suspect) many genres of human communication. This explains Conquergood's insistence that engaged scholarship and activism must take into account "the embodied dynamics that constitute meaningful human interaction" by striving for "a hermeneutics of experience, copresence, humility, and vulnerability." Recent literature on ethnography and performance studies has demonstrated the many ways these imperatives may be pursued, often with stunning results, yet I fear that much of this work has tended to fall into a troubling pattern of sensationalism and narcissism, celebrating the raw immediacy of personal experience over any attempt to make structural sense of the larger historical, political, and cultural conditions surrounding daily life. As ever, then, the methodological conundrum is striving to balance the self and society, text and context, the existential delirium of the now with the scholarly rigor of analysis. This is not the place for an extended meditation on these methodological questions; suffice it to say that I strive in the investigative prison poems that follow to celebrate the embodied, existentially unfiltered wonder of daily life while always striving to speak from these experiences outward to the larger historical, political, and cultural conditions that infuse even the most mundane acts with deep significance. Indeed, by interweaving analyses of cultural symbolism, class privilege, rhetorical criticism, and imaginative flights of fancy, all the while foregrounding my personal experiences with the dignity of prisoners and activists alike, and all the while clinging to the power of beauty—especially in the face of terror—I hope my investigative prison poetry lives up to and perhaps even expands the visions of engaged scholarship offered by Conquergood, Frey, Bourdieu, and Scarry.[7]

*   *   *   *   *

Ginsberg had insight
but we've seen the truth:
there are few best minds
left

> at least in *this* prison—
> & anyone planning to howl
> must soon discover the sound
> doesn't reach attentive ears.[8]

Prison Poets, Empowering Editors, & Critical Criminologists

> This world is flat
> The closer I get to the edge
> The more I think of jumping
> Freefall into oblivion
> A comet in the night sky[9]

Thus David Bowman, a prisoner in North Carolina, imagines throwing himself off the face of the planet only to be reborn as a comet streaking across the sky—but of course he need not engage in such dramatic activity, for in describing his oscillation from the despair of oblivion to the thrill of transcendence Bowman has, like so many imprisoned poets before him, made the more tangible leap into the dignity of authorship. Readers who have not worked in, been sentenced to, or had loved ones locked up in prisons may find it hard to imagine how truly life-saving that leap is for imprisoned writers. The women of the Bedford Hills Writing Workshop, run in the Bedford Hills Correctional Facility in New York by Hettie Jones, captured the importance of this leap into the dignity of authorship in a collectively authored poem depicting their

> reaching for words
>
> like fruit, like stars, words
> to save their lives
> to snatch them from the streets
> defend their dreams . . .
>
> to change our lives[10]

The switching of pronouns from "their" to "our" shows how in writing the women have moved closer to owning their own words, their own dreams, their own lives. In fact, for as long as the Western world has relied on prisons, prisoners have sought solace and redemption in writing. This has been especially true in America, where the flood of writings coming out of our nation's embarrassing number of prisons has been so voluminous and so creative that it amounts to, in H. Bruce Franklin's estimate, "One of the most extraordinary achievements of twentieth-century American culture." Anyone who doubts that claim should look at Franklin's most recent collection of twentieth century American prison writings, which includes pieces by, among many others, Jack London, Kate Richards O'Hare, Chester Himes, Nelson Algren, Robert Lowell, Malcolm X, Jack Henry Abbott, Malcolm Braly, Ethridge Knight, Jimmy Santiago Baca, Edward Bunker, and Mumia Abu-Jamal. I have never been imprisoned and have not known the desperate lives endured by many of these authors, and so am obviously writing from a space of privilege and comfort that is foreign to this class of imprisoned writers. Nonetheless, I claim them as my teachers, as my models of how to write politically, as my inspirations for speaking truth to power. The investigative prison poems contained herein thus hope both to honor and expand that long line of writings about America's prisons.[11]

The imprisoned writers noted above would not be known to the world today were it not for the tireless efforts of a group of what I call empowering editors. Like Franklin, Bell Gale Chevigny—the editor of the collection including the poem about self-discovery quoted above—and Marilla Arguelles—editor of *Extracts from Pelican Bay*, a chilling book of poems from California's most brutal supermax prison—scholars and writers around the nation have dedicated their lives to making sure the work of imprisoned writers reaches broad audiences. Sometimes these empowering editors are prisoners themselves, as in the case of Wilbert Rideau and Ron Wikberg, men who edited both *The Angolite*, the magazine produced from within the Angola State Prison, and *Life Sentences: Rage and Survival Behind Bars*, a powerful collection of prisoner writings. Frequently writers who merge teaching, publishing, activism, and their own creative works, these empowering editors deserve our highest praise, for without them we would not only have no prison literature, but the community of prison activists would be deprived of one of its most persuasive weapons: the words of incarcerated men and women. For example, the lines from Bowman quoted above were published in *Correction(s)*, a new journal of prisoner writings edited by Katie Adams. Katie lives in the East Village, where she is a Doctoral candidate writing a dissertation on the history of prison litera-

ture, a for-hire workout guru, a teacher who shares her knowledge of poetry with prisoner-students, and an activist. I had the good fortune in
June 2002 to spend a long weekend at the Blue Mountain Arts Center in
upstate New York, where I had the joyous experience of watching Katie
talk about prison poetry with Dick Shelton. Dick lives in Tucson, from
where he has been writing up a storm and running poetry workshops for
Arizona's prisoners for longer than Katie has been alive. Like Katie,
Dick edits a journal of prisoner writings, entitled *Walking Rain Review*;
like *Correction(s)*, *Walking Rain Review* offers readers a stunning opportunity to share the humanity of some of the men and women locked
up in the prison-industrial-complex. Our conversations that weekend
were enriched by the staccato energy of Tory Samartino, a twenty-
something hipster who teaches poetry to the juvies doing time on Rikers
Island. All nervous energy and youthful fury, Tory runs *Voices Unbroken*, a teaching, publishing, and activist group that fills our world with
the hip hop energies of the lost children who grew up in the slums encir-
cling Manhattan. I was thankful that weekend as well for the contributions of Raylene Hinz-Penner, a Mennonite professor of English at
Bethel College, out on the plains of Kansas, where she teaches poetry at
the Hutchinson Correctional Facility. Calm and soft-spoken, filling those
around her with a sense of comfort and ease, Raylene edits a sweet little
pamphlet of prisoner writings called *Out of The Blue Book*, which opens
with Raylene's mantra:

> Just here and now,
> no one knows our crime
>   or how much time.
> Around this table,
>   we just write,
>   (we, just right).[12]

We just write/right, indeed, for as Franklin, Chevigny, Arguelles,
Wikberg and Rideau, Adams, Shelton, Samartino, Hinz-Penner, and the
hundreds of other empowering editors around the country have learned,
imprisoned writers frequently find writing a special process of self-
discovery. Often drying out after long years of alcoholism and/or addiction, frequently full of guilt and self-loathing from prior lives of anger
and danger, and usually hailing from neighborhoods that offered few
educational opportunities, an incredible number of imprisoned writers

seem to first fully comprehend their own humanity, their own potential, and the harm they have caused others when engaged in writing work-shops that encourage them to dig deeper into themselves than they ever have before. Ask any of these empowering editors and they will tell you that writing workshops in prisons take on cathartic, truly redemptive en-ergies—hence the power and passion of so much prison writing. I have tried to honor this tradition of empowering editors by including in the poems published here the words of my imprisoned students and other imprisoned writers, hence amplifying the voices of those who have been habitually silenced. Marshaling the words of prisoners is but one small way that I try throughout this book to continue that tradition of empow-ering editors, and hence to practice what Carolyn Forché refers to as the need "everywhere and always / to go after that which is lost."[13]

Many of the empowering editors mentioned above will also tell you, however, that even those of us who can walk out of prisons after a long night of teaching find ourselves haunted by prisons. Sister Helen Prejean, author of *Dead Man Walking* and a hero to those of us active in the fight against the death penalty, writes that "At the end of each [prison] visit I get to walk out. And every time I find myself taking deep gulps of free-dom." But as Prejean and others who work in prisons know well, you cannot live in close proximity to terror without reconsidering the costs of freedom. Hence Bruce Franklin has spent much of his life trying to fig-ure out in elegant written works and powerful lectures how the legacy of slavery and the practices of racism drive the prison-industrial-complex. Hence Joe Bruchac has spent over three decades writing and performing pieces that try to fathom how the destruction of indigenous Indian and folk cultures is linked to the rise of prisons. Hence Judith Tannenbaum has spent the past thirty years learning how to merge her work as teacher, poet, and activist, ultimately deciding "to give up willful pretense, and to live an unmasked life of surrender." I understand Tannenbaum to mean here that her imprisoned students cannot open up and share their works with her until she opens up and shares with them—hence pushing her toward a life of radical sincerity, where irony, pretense, and affect give way to the more important work of teaching well, writing well, and ad-vocating well. But "an unmasked life of surrender" also means recog-nizing that all your best efforts may make little headway against the seemingly relentless power of the prison-industrial-complex. So the trick, Tannenbaum is telling us, is to hold onto hope while practicing humility. The problem, of course, is that it is daunting to realize that democracy is confounded in every direction by the prison-industrial-complex; it is haunting to know that some of your students will die in prison and that others will be killed there; it is maddening to learn that your students in the university have to work extra hours at lousy jobs so they can pay for tuition hikes triggered by the state education budget getting slashed due to increased prison spending; it is paralyzing to suspect that years and years of commitment in the end may amount to nothing—and on and on in a swirling chain of doubt and frustration. What Prejean, Franklin, Bruchac, Tannenbaum and others have thus learned is that one cannot work in the shadow of prisons without finding a way of making peace with the demons of doubt and frustration. The poems in this volume are best approached, then, not as aberrations within the world of letters, but as part of a hundreds-of-years-old tradition of writings from and about prison, and as part of the more recent flood of writings by those of us who work in prisons and need to try to make sense of the relationships among our lives as free people, our work as teachers and activists, and our experiences in prisons. Ultimately, these two traditions offer readers rich opportunities for thinking not only about prisons but about the complicated ways race, class, crime, and violence have shaped the practices of democracy in America.[14]

A third strand of important work represented in the poems included herein is that body of critical criminology produced by scholars concerned with revealing the intricacies of the prison-industrial-complex. Some of these works are historical studies that tackle the foreground to our current dilemma, including David Rothman's *The Discovery of the Asylum*, Michel Foucault's *Discipline and Punish*, and Karen Halttunen's *Murder Most Foul*; some of them focus on cultural questions about the production of images about criminals, including Marie Christine Leps' *Apprehending the Criminal* and John Sloop's *The Cultural Prison*; some of them examine the economics of incarceration, including Nils Christie's *Crime Control as Industry*, Jeffrey Reiman's *The Rich Get Richer and the Poor Get Prison*, and David Shichor's *Punishment for Profit*; and others of them are written in a spirit of muckraking journalism, including Daniel Burton-Roses' collection of essays on *The Celling of America*, Steven Donziger and the National Criminal Justice Commission's *The Real War on Crime*, and Christian Parenti's *Lockdown America*. What these books share is a commitment to the power of evidence: all of them rely on an overwhelming number of research sources, which pile on top of one another forming a crushing weight of proof. The following poems depend on these and other sources for supplying such proof, thus enhancing the experiential power of the poems by suffusing them with evidence gleaned from our best historians and criminologists.[15]

Having thus celebrated the work of activists, engaged intellectuals, imprisoned writers, empowering editors, and critical criminologists, the question remains how to bring them together into one seamless genre. Unfortunately, I know of no text that does so regarding prisons. Luckily, though, John Dos Passos, Carolyn Forché, and Peter Dale Scott have shown how this merging of genres may work, albeit while tackling different concerns. Nonetheless, I offer below a brief reading of some of their work in the hope that doing so will enable readers to appreciate the reading and writing practices that inform the investigative prison poems included here.

Three Models of Investigative Poetry: Dos Passos, Forché, & Scott

Readers interested in aesthetic theory will be familiar with the long tradition of arguments regarding the possibilities of weaving political and historical material into works of art.[16] I will not bore readers with a recap of those traditions, but I will address briefly three models I have found useful for thinking about ways to produce political art. First among these models is John Dos Passos's *U.S.A.* trilogy, consisting of *The 42nd Parallel* (1930), *Nineteen Nineteen* (1932), and *The Big Money* (1936).[17] The bulk of these sprawling novels consists of traditional narratives following the misadventures of characters confronted with the various economic, cultural, and political complications following from the manic boom-and-bust cycles of unregulated capitalism and America's entry into World War I. Each story is followed, however, by short sections entitled Newsreels, The Camera Eye, and poetic biographies of the period's key players. The Newsreels consist of newspaper headlines, snippets of newspaper stories, and snatched refrains from popular songs—*Oh say can you see . . .* (p. 248)*; Where do we go from here, boys?* (p. 195). Arrayed on the page as a string of disconnected shards of evidence, these Newsreels provide an eerie glimpse into the world of popular culture, mass-produced misinformation, and the vast majority of events that have simply fallen into historical oblivion.

The Newsreels are followed by Camera Eye sections in which Dos Passos offers disjointed observations, literally camera shots of turmoil. In this case we watch the angry response of socialists in Paris to the Treaty of Versailles: "at the République   à bass la guerre MORT AUX VACHES à bas le Paix de Assassins   they've torn up the gratings from around the trees and are throwing stones and bits of castirons at the fancydressed Republican Guards hissing whistling poking at the horses with umbrellas   scraps of the *International*" (p. 396-7). As indicated by the random gaps in the passages quoted above, the confusion of who is speaking, and the bristling sense of confused immediacy, these sections frequently fade into stream-of-consciousness, thus offering readers glimpses into the fractured experience of living daily life amidst epochal historical transformations. Dos Passos follows these blasts of existential confusion with poetic biographies, from which I have taken this verse on Randolph S. Bourne:

> This little sparrow like man
> tiny twisted bit of flesh in a black cape,
> always in pain and ailing,
> put a pebble in his sling
> and hit Goliath in the forehead with it
> *War*, he wrote, *is the health of the state* (p. 120)

Made popular in Howard Zinn's magnificent *A People's History of the United States*, Bourne's phrase has stood for generations as an indictment of U.S militarism. By chronicling the struggles of this largely forgotten figure, Dos Passos's melancholy biographical poem enriches our sense of American history, making it more somber and personal.[18]

The combination of the explanatory narratives, the evidence-offering Newsreels, the existentially rich Camera Eye sections, and the poetic biographies offers readers four perspectives from which to approach history. The more I have read and taught Dos Passos, however, the more I have come to view the narratives as unnecessary bridges linking the more experimental parts of the trilogy. The investigative poems that follow are thus, in large part, attempts to practice a Dos Passos-like aesthetic minus the narratives; instead of a traditional novel weaving around experimental subsections, I have tried to combine the power of Newsreels, Camera Eyes, and poetic biographies, all the while filling the text with historical materials that erupt into the present. This explains why in the poems that follow readers are asked to leap with me from conversations between prisoners and guards to debates between Abraham Lincoln and Steven Douglas, from contemporary criminological policy debates to nineteenth century arguments over phrenology, from anti-death penalty meetings at the Oakland YWCA to the antebellum antislavery position of Daniel Webster (the statesman after whom the street upon which the YWCA sits was named), and so on. In short, playing with Dos Passos-like forms of writing has led me to try to merge traditional historiographical and experimental literary methods of thinking historically, thus enabling me to approach the deep structural integrity of history while holding onto the sense of awestruck wonder and confusion that fills each small moment of time.[19]

A second important model of textual production influencing the poems included here is provided by Carolyn Forché's *The Country Between Us* (1981) and *The Angel of History* (1994). Based on her journalistic work in El Salvador during the height of that country's civil war, *The Country Between Us* offers a model for a poetry of witness in which the poet is not only a chronicler of hope and terror but also a participant in the processes she examines. The poems in this remarkable book thus veer from scalding political critiques of Salvadoran tyrants to self-implicating ruminations on how even the most mundane pleasures in the United States bear the stain of the violence our government funds in the third world. Like so many of us who find that our work in prisons changes the ways we think about freedom, so Forché finds that living in close proximity to barbarism in El Salvador casts shadows across daily space. She is thus unnerved by the sense of decadence and ease signaled by "the iced drinks and paper umbrellas, clean / toilets and Los Angeles palm trees moving / like lean women." Like so many of us, she finds the happy ignorance of many Americans regarding the brutality their country foists on the world unbearable. Speaking to a friend, she laments:

> you were born to an island of greed
> and grace where you have the sense
> of yourself as apart from others. It is
> not your right to feel powerless. Better
> people than you were powerless.[20]

Many of these better people appear in the pages of *The Angel of History*, where Forché expands her poetry of witness to encompass the

European Holocaust and the impact of the Unites States dropping nuclear bombs on Japan. Taking her title from the well known story told in Walter Benjamin's "Theses on the Philosophy of History," where an angel is blown backward into the future while watching the present produce an ever-growing pile of wreckage, Forché tackles the horrors of World War II in personal poems full of stories of her lost relatives and friends. While leading readers on this personally inflected historical journey into barbarism, Forché speculates—frequently through the voices of other writers and philosophers—on the possibilities of forgiveness. *The Angel of History* is therefore less an investigative attempt to name names and pinpoint causes than a philosophical attempt to make sense of the persistence of hope in the face of unspeakable suffering. Aphoristic and enigmatic—and hence almost impossible to quote without including pages of supporting material—the poems accumulate power from their many references to other texts, hence offering readers less a definitive statement than a series of beautiful theses, each equipped with what amounts to a list of suggested readings. Thus, while embodying the wonder and openness of elegant poetry, *Angel of History* stands ultimately as a pedagogical tool for wondering what it means to cherish art in an age of destruction.[21]

The third and by far the most important model influencing the investigative prison poems printed here is offered by Peter Dale Scott's *Seculum* trilogy. The first part of the trilogy, *Coming to Jakarta: A Poem about Terror* (1988), has been lauded in *The Boston Review* as "remarkable and unnerving"; in London's *Times Literary Supplement* as "a work of great richness and complexity"; in *Parnassus* as "revolutionary"; and, in a special issue of *AGNI*, by no less a national hero than the Poet Laureate Robert Hass, as "the most important political poem to appear in the English language in a very long time." Like these enthusiastic reviewers, I have been deeply impressed by the sophistication and depth of Scott's political analysis, the epic sweep of his historical knowledge, the revelatory honesty of his self-implicating poems, and the sheer beauty of his verse. By interweaving these four qualities—political acumen, historical grounding, self-reflexivity, and poetic beauty—Scott produces what I call *an interdisciplinary aesthetics of provisional eloquence*. That is, by merging the four qualities noted above, and by doing so while confronting a political calamity, Scott provides us with an empowering, elegant example of the search for grace amidst terror.[22]

Coming to Jakarta was triggered by Scott's need to write "about the 1965 massacre / of Indonesians by Indonesians" (p. 24) while simultaneously questioning his own complicity—as poet, professor, one-time diplomat, father, husband, and activist—in the events that led to the CIA-sponsored butchery of over 500,000 Indonesian "communists" following the coup that replaced Sukarno with Suharto.[23] For example, in the second poem of *Jakarta* we find Scott suffering from

> the uprising in my stomach
>> against so much good food and
> wine America or was it

> giving one last broadcast too many
>> about the Letelier assassins
> the heroin traffic

> a subject I no longer hope
>> to get a handle on (p. 10).[24]

These lines depict Scott as an activist/intellectual speaking publicly about the subterranean links between assassination politics and the drug war, as a typical over-consumer gorged on too much decadence, and as a consummate researcher who, suffering from the nausea brought on by too much familiarity with evil, wishes that the facts would mysteriously vanish into the comforting oblivion of ignorance—but of course they do not.[25] Instead, history forces itself mercilessly onto Scott, prodding him to engage in a relentless pursuit of *evidence*, dragging him deeper and deeper into both the psychology and political-economy of terror:

> Already we are descending
> into these shadows which

> hang about as if there
>> were something much more urgent
> left wholly unsaid (p. 13).

Readers interested in the facts of the Indonesian massacre will find over one-hundred sources listed in Scott's notes, which situate Suharto's coup and the ensuing anticommunist genocide within the overlapping politico-economic framework of post-World War II international finance, the transition from modern, empire- and ideologically-driven colonialism into the postmodern neocolonialism of multinational corporations, underground think tanks, and globe-trotting mercenaries, and the continuing subversion of democratic politics at the behest of the global caste-bound thugs who run secret governments as if they were their own private shooting galleries for aristocratic sportsmen. The research used to document these charges is breathtaking, thus offering readers a tutorial in how to pursue interdisciplinary political criticism. As the poet and critic Ed Sanders wrote in his 1976 manifesto, *Investigative Poetry*, in a passage celebrating Ezra Pound (a figure who haunts the pages of Scott's work as well), "the essence of investigative poetry" is to create "lines of lyric beauty [that] descend from data clusters," hence both seducing and empowering readers with "a melodic blizzard of data-fragments."[26]

But whereas such melodic blizzards may leave many readers baffled, or at the least searching for personal relevance in such waves of "data clusters," Scott weaves his remarkable research around and through moments of daily life, hence showing us how power courses through even the most mundane activities. For example, watch below as Scott links the disparate strands of the international political-economy of terror, U.S. weapons manufacturers, Indonesian and Saudi tycoons, the refuse of Nixon's henchmen, and the friendly neighborhood bank:

> and I thought of Adnan Khashoggi
> > the Indonesian shipping magnate
> > Saudi friend of Pak
>
> Chung Hee and Roy Furmak
> > *$106 million*
> > in Lockheed commissions
>
> to Khashoggi alone
> > and twice that
> > amount withdrawn by Khashoggi
>
> from Rebozo's bank in Key Biscayne
> > in May and November '72
> > and of Lim Suharto's *cukong*

> who has bought the Hibernian bank
> with a branch on the Berkeley campus
> from profits on arms deals (pps. 127-128).

Scott's awesome courage in exposing the shadowy operatives and off-shore bankers and behind-the-scenes boardroom connections that fuel imperialism, in conjunction with his sweeping grasp of history and his uncanny ability to render such topics in recognizable terms—*a branch on the Berkeley campus*—render *Coming to Jakarta* a world-class example of historical and political analysis.

In fact, only recently, more than ten years after the publication of *Jakarta*, has the mainstream media finally begun to address the underworld U.S./Indonesia connections first exposed in Scott's poem. For example, it is now known that Freeport MacMoRan, Texaco, Mobil, Raytheon, Hughes Aircraft, and Merrill Lynch (among others) are major financial sponsors of the U.S./Indonesia Society, a lobbying group co-chaired by Reagan's Secretary of State, George Schultz, and featuring James Riady as a trustee and John Huang as a consultant. Thus two of the central figures (Riady and Huang) in one of the Democratic Party campaign finance scandals that rocked the Clinton presidency turned out to be significant U.S./Indonesia Society figures. Eyal Press observed at the time that the Society was "a public relations organ for the Suharto regime." Hence, beneath the surface scandal of the Democratic National Party accepting illegal foreign campaign contributions, journalists found the much deeper scandal of continuing links between Suharto's brutal regime, U.S.-based transnationals, and the U.S. government. That Scott's *Jakarta* exposed these connections ten years before the mainstream press would even consider them demonstrates the remarkable depth and courage of the poem's political and historical analysis. Using Scott's *Jakarta* as a model, then, the investigative poems published here attempt to use rigorous research to name names, to show who owns what and whom, and thus to lay bare the institutional and economic structures propping up the prison-industrial-complex.[27]

Scott's work is just as impressive, however, as an experiment in reconstructing a new and problematic sense of an endlessly compromised self in the face of terror. Hence Scott's revelation that

> To have learnt from terror
> to see oneself

as part of the enemy

can be a reassurance
whatever it is
arises within us (p. 62).

Like Dos Passos and Forché, then, Scott's poems perform a dialectical interweaving of perspectives: each well-documented scene of political barbarism segues into personal observations on the nature of complicity; each personal rumination on complicity fades into questions of commitment and the historical obligation of engaged citizens to at least attempt to speak truth to power; each engagement with the numbing expanse of global power politics in turn leads back to the suspicion that perhaps grace can only be found, after all, amidst those moments when daily life is lived as an aesthetic experience. Thus the prevalence in *Listening to the Candle*, the second part of the *Seculum* trilogy, of simple pleasures

focused on the mysteries
of dailiness

baking bread on Saturdays
smelling the freshness
of sun-dried laundry

while you fold the sheet
against yourself
from the garden line[28]

Later in the poem, after chronicling the December 1980 murder of American evangelicals working with peasants in El Salvador, Scott suggests that

in such a time it is still good

having danced until midnight
to Mika's and John's new band
after the family lasagna

> all generations
>> our children and their friends
>> dancing together singly (*Candle*, 106)

Terror and grace therefore jostle each other within the infinitely textured particulars of the day:

> From the Bay Bridge
>> on the way home from the opera
>> you could look down on the searchlights

> of the Oakland Army Terminal
>> where they loaded the containers
>> of pellet-bombs and napalm (*Jakarta*, 103)

Although not about prisons per se, I can think of no better way of approaching a world haunted at every turn by them, for in the images above Scott shows us how even the drive home from the opera, that quintessential marker of high art, leads one past places of mass-produced violence. *If you look around*, Scott tells us, *you will find yourself implicated in things you have previously spent a great deal of time and energy pretending not to recognize.*

These epiphanic moments of realization need not be paralyzing however, as Scott shows us again and again how to channel them into a renewed commitment to work not only politically for peace and justice but also personally for something approaching kindness. In fact, in *Minding the Darkness*, the third volume of the *Seculum* trilogy, Scott turns increasingly to Buddhism as a way of practicing what he calls mindfulness. While Scott's turn to Buddhism is woven throughout the book, he demonstrates its challenges and opportunities most explicitly in four poems chronicling Buddhist retreats. In contrast to the scathing investigative poetry of *Jakarta* and the meditative work in *Candle*, *Darkness* thus demonstrates a middle way of mindful politics, of both critique and contemplation. Although the word has fallen into disrepute, and for good reason given the many cranks and hucksters making their living off of its marketing, one is tempted to say that this turn to Buddhism illustrates Scott's hankering less for the smoking gun that will rip away the lies of any given regime than the *wisdom* that will help him live amidst so much waste and cruelty. Indeed, by tracking down his footnotes, by rambling

through his childhood traumas and parental pleasures, by forcing ourselves to confront both his and our complicity with the global carnage of
low intensity anticommunism, unabashed designer capitalism, and the
pleasures of high culture, by making paratactical leaps from fragmentary
images and quotations toward our own approximate understanding of the
text, and by enthusiastically embodying a turn towards Buddhist values,
Scott teaches attentive readers to treat the poem as a heuristic device.
The mysterious "something much more urgent / left wholly unsaid" (*Jakarta*, 13) appears here to be the realization that poetry—as trigger for
research, as source of grace, as means of confronting terror, as process of
self-critique and reconstruction—amounts to a self-regenerating process
in which, as Scott said in an interview, "one works through personal resistance and disempowerment to re-empowerment."[29]

I am reminded here of Terrence Des Pres's comment in a roundtable
discussion on the possibilities of political poetry that

> we turn where we can for sustenance, and some of us
> take poetry seriously in exactly this way. . . [W]hen it
> comes to the Bomb, or just to the prospect of empires in
> endless conflict, it seems clear we cannot do very much
> very fast. So the immediate question isn't what to do but
> *how to live*, and some of us, at least, turn for help to po-
> etry.[30]

The sustenance of *Coming to Jakarta*, *Listening to the Candle*, and
Minding the Darkness derives from the pleasures of sharing one's burden
as an informed and engaged citizen in a rapidly unraveling democracy
while not devolving into solipsism, cynicism, or madness. Hence Scott's
prudent advice in the closing section of *Jakarta*:

> As for those of us
>   who are lucky enough
>   not to sit hypnotized
>
>   our hands on the steering wheel
>   which seems to have detached itself
>   from the speeding vehicle

it is our job to say
    relax trust
spend more time with your children

things can only go
    a little better
if you do not hang on so hard (p. 129)

*   *   *   *   *

In prison you put on your clothes
and take them off again.
You jam your food down
and shit it out again.
You round the compound right
to left and right again.[31]

Reading Investigative Prison Poems

Having celebrated Dos Passos's *U.S.A.* trilogy, Forché's poetry of witness, and Scott's investigative poetry as models of how to merge historical materials, political analysis, investigative muckraking, self-exploration, and poetry, I closed the section above with a jarring juxtaposition, following Scott's words of hope and prudence with Father Daniel Berrigan's bleak portrayal of the monotony of prison life. The poems that follow are full of such juxtapositions, thus asking readers to work the gaps between hope and despair on their own—I tend not to fill these spaces so much as to create them, hopefully enticing readers to do the hard work of interpretation.

These juxtapositions of perspective are generally indicated typographically, by a verse being tabbed in or out from the one above it: such tabbings indicate breaks in time, space, or voice. These breaks render the poems difficult to follow, especially when they enable the past to erupt into the present. For example, in the poems included here on San Quentin Prison, readers are asked to approach 1850s San Francisco as if it were yesterday; in the poems on the death penalty, readers are asked to hear slave beatings while thinking of botched executions; and so the dead are made to speak, the past is made alive, the absent is made present. As

Forché argues in the Introduction to *Against Forgetting*, "The poetry of witness frequently resorts to paradox and difficult equivocation, to the invocation of what is *not* there as if it *were*. . . . That it must defy common sense to speak of the common indicates that traditional modes of thought, the purview of common sense, no longer *make* sense."[32]

Wherever the many voices mentioned throughout this introduction appear in the text they are indicated by italics. When I perform these poems I ask friends to read these lines, hence creating an audible sense of shifting voice. Readers are thus encouraged to think of these poems and their strangely italicized lines almost as reading scripts—or as what Ed Sanders called "high energy verse grids"—that are best read aloud with theatrical energy. Some of these lines are paraphrases of conversations with students, prison guards, and other sources who have chosen to remain anonymous, but the vast majority of them are direct quotations which are footnoted, hence enabling interested readers to track down my sources. Such secondary work is by no means necessary for enjoying the poems, but it will certainly provide energetic readers with a much richer sense of the materials at hand. Finally, I hope readers will notice that even as these poems document the prison-industrial-complex's mass-production of brutality, so they cling to the hope that the voices celebrated here are well on their way not only to dismantling that hellish system but ultimately to redeeming the practices of democracy in America. For as Daniel Berrigan reminds us, "as we hope, we are."[33]

PENDLETON POEMS

For Jon Rutter, Steve Guy, and my students in
the Indiana Reformatory and the Indiana Correctional Facility

Punishment
is the most potent stimulus
of violence
nothing corrodes the soul
as thoroughly as
vengeance[1]

I. *Students*

Black separatists little Africas
        dangling from their necks
    command the back corner

eyeing the Muslims
        soft-spoken Mahdi Buddy-Love
    prayer mats unrolled

kneeling eastward imagining
        life beyond guard towers
    35' walls motion sensors

    parking lot of pick-ups armed
            with rifle racks nudie mud flaps
        NRA bumper stickers *Let's GO*

Colts! rifle range across the train tracks
        cracks echoing through golden Autumn
    fields damp fallen leaves giant hay bales

upturned black soil filling the crisp air
        with sweet suggestions of plenitude
    bullets exploding *crack* into inner circles

of imagined runaways *bull's-eye*
        before class at The Post *Hey Cheryl*
  —Stew—how's the pumpkin pie?

I'll take some'a that Joe so weak *crack*
        Eric supplements his pre-class jolt
  with one-shot *crack* coffee bags

while reviewing notes on Kant *crack*
        Jon leafing through Chomsky *Afternoon*
  fellas—hey Cheryl—teach 'em good

onwards to Mecca *crack* dignity
        freedom *the real threat of prison*
  is to the integrity of expression[2]

    at the lukewarm water fountain
        Wolfy on fire with Marx Jefferson
    I entered prison as a fifteen year old

    with less than a ninth grade education
      I had attempted suicide
    turned away the love
        of my family and friends
          I had given up on life[3]

    now Wolfy so eager
      to learn so hungry
    slowly recognizing his gifts

    thinking caring writing
      becoming a leader
    his essays published

in *The Prison News Service*
        calling his peers to *expose ideologies*
    to *deconstruct rationalizations*[4]

Kris reading poems of forgiveness
        in a hushed voice
    brushing back his long blonde hair

as hardened men gulp
        holding back tears
    while Kris promises

In love I trust
        The sacred field
    of reverence is all

    I need to be
            found in who
        I am becoming

willingly excited by imperfection
        forgiven the misery of existence
    awakened to a world possibility[5]

shouting over the factory
        whistle screaming obedience
    lunch shift in rec. shift out

end of break *all right gentlemen*
        let's begin again let's begin
    again laughing tattooed bikers

now clean sharing drug adventures
        beneath the table of elements
    hanging precariously above

the non-aligned students prisoners
stuffed into high school desks
        dreaming out windows welded shut

choking on clouds of chalk
      swept from black boards
so old the corners crumble

brittle erasers churning ashes
      into air so dry I gasp for breath
stumbling onto *the intractable*

   thereness of what time made[6]
      reeling from the stifling ugliness
   of gray walls gray clothing gray

   food gray soul gray dismal
      gray no bright colors
   no music no laughter no beauty[7]

   save the genius of perseverance
      Daniel Berrigan praying through
   the pukehued mockery of hope[8]

I lurch back into time falling
      through multiplicity reaching
for a question to steady the world

   Tinnin-Bey tell us please
      what Dr. Arendt might say
   about the dialectic of violence and power?

father grandfather brother friend
      speaking gently long fingers tracing
circles in the air book pages dog-eared

   I believe if we turn to page 110
      we'll find the sister claiming
   "rage is the form in which

misfortune becomes
active it is impotent
the last stages of despair"[9]

—like last night when the youngsters
in F-dorm threw down
over the Nebraska game?

Big Will making connections
Wolfy the prodigy
nineteen year old monster

absorbing books ideas
visions guilt killing him
Tinnin-Bey nailed it

check out the handout Page 153
"The loss of power becomes
a temptation to substitute

violence for power"[10]
our conversation slowly
approaching some grace

some tentative plateau
of understanding
shaping the hope

to begin again

II. *Jailers*

It's easy to pretend
I don't pay rent
to the conspiracies[11]

yet I must confess
        no greater satisfaction
   than fleeing that shit hole

dungeon gulag factory
        of *fallingrief of unpleasure*[12]
   designed to humiliate

   I shuffle through double-doored
          electric sally ports buzzers
      triggered behind bulletproof glass

      tear them all down
            address the irrational
        need to inflict revenge[13]

   x-ray machines video cameras
          open your bag gotta pat you down
   drug dogs sniffing my crotch

   potential threat to security *fuckin' A*
          Bobby Knight can't win no more
      Keady's got the athletes now

them city kids wanna' run-n-gun
        that disciplined game is dead
   fuckin' UNLV could beat the Knicks

   I've found if I talk sports
        the guards go easy
     on the obligatory harassment

   Officer B. even using his slapjack
        glad to help the day I locked
   my keys on *crack* the front seat

   Thank you officer—don't sweat it
        that's what we're about here crack
   community solidarity brotherhood

the simple truth
> we could be friends
> neighbors jogging partners

sharing daily joys
> mind wandering at work
> like the Quentin tower guard

> who *dips his rifle*
> > *then raises it again*
> > *dreamily he imagines*

> *a speckled trout*
> > *coming up shining*
> > *and raging with life*[14]

but for the pressure to inflict
> pain damaging the guards
> as much as the prisoners

the temptation so great
> to abuse the impunity
> of unchecked power

guard culture so klanish
> defining honor through cruelty
> dehumanizing others themselves

> we know guard violence
> > is *neither idiosyncratic*
> > *nor a form of self-defense*

> but *a socially structured tactic*
> > *entrenched* not for maintaining order
> > but as the only route

of *upward mobility* prestige
> belonging and power
within the officers' corps[15]

I've never seen any guard violence
> only read about it talked about it
my students telling stories on break

my conversations with guards
> walking across the yard through security
none as sad as in the vending lounge

guards slump in blue plastic chairs
> talk of fishing bowling high school
football *nice barbecue Jeremy*

after too long shifts winding down
> hats and belts off smoking cigarettes
drinking Diet Pepsi eating chips cookies

trading stories of slamming Jeffries'
> face into the wall *that son of a bitch*
or the crew on the cell extraction

broke Thompson's arm while he was cuffed
> *the report'll be clean Stew promised*
Nice job Sammy—you 'da man Ralph

Mother-fucker tried to block your punch
> *I caught him low with the baton*
d'you see the Sergeant smile?

but mostly just job talk
> about lousy bosses *I got*
the fuckin' 3 shift again

lousy pay lousy wives lousy husbands
> *fuckin' kid was smokin' my cigarettes*
drinkin' my beers payin' no rent

his teacher says
> *he needs more attention*
> *I'll fuckin' give him attention*

—go soft man he's just a kid
> *look at Ann she came around*
> *goin' to State in the Fall*

—he's right Pat
> *you don't wanna*
> *come down too hard*

he might snap
> *you never know*
> *he could do something crazy*

—listen to you both damn
> *the kid's just playin'*
> *it's not like he's*

a criminal or something

III. *Friends*

History from 12:30-3:15
> then hang in the libes
with the guys filing cases

Billy bummed by Lincoln's waffling
> *man he copped out at Alton*
dig this "irrespective of the moral question . . .

I am still in favor
> *of the new territory*
> *being kept free*
>> *into which white men*
>> *may move"*[16]

Billy holding his book high
> *getting some education*
basically saved me[17]

shoulders shaking free
> hand slamming the table
guards look over annoyed

and he says it again later
> *here dig this*
talkin' 'bout the frontier

being "an outlet for
> *the free white people"*[18]
I am unraveled recoiling

Susan How echoing
> in my mind *the past is*
present we are all part

of the background
> *what if then*
is now?[19]

Billy mercifully laughs
> *that's too much*
grabs my shoulder

centering propelling me
> down the hallway to teach
the Drug War from 3:30-6:15

then route 69 to Muncie 332
> the forgotten back way
past abandoned farms

playing class over and over
      Solomon playfully livid
you gotta be kiddin' me

man this is unreal
      "the CIA gave Noriega $332,226
as an informant"?[20]

    past the junk-yard tractors
        car windows shattered
    from buckshot beebees

    wild corn sprouting
        through engine blocks
    piles of tires mulching

    squirrels diving for cover
        in the empty cutlery
    tray of a dishwasher

Greg tired of life
    grandfather in for coke
I was outta control

now clean confident
    our program coordinator
4.0 GPA

peeking out from a stack of photocopies
    smiling in recognition *"Being-*
in-the-world has lost itself

in inertia it encounters
    radical insufficiency yet
can't let go instead *increasing*

the level of dependency
    in a kind of vertigo
of endless repetition" damn[21]

that's exactly right that's it
I was there perhaps I
should reconsider Heidegger

after all Friday night radio
talk about my Cardinals
Ball State should hammer Toledo

yes sir our ground game's been clicking
through blocks of boarded-up shops
to Jon's place on Wheeling

beside the White River meandering
beneath towering light banks
casting bug-filled shadows

the high school football half-time
marching band's train wreck
floats over the sycamores

landing gently amidst our talk
on Jon's sagging porch
with beers brown rice veggies

Michael said he might drop by
—how's he doing keeping clean?
—I believe not doin' too well in French

Jon's world clean honest good
food good music good books
been teaching in prisons for years

helping guys make the transition
giving more than he can afford
building *a fellowship of learning*[22]

we spend the night talking
about classes trading stories
notes citations listening to music

Michael comes by with a friend
        dubious stoned *this ain't cool man*
    you gotta be straight—hit the books

—don't fuck this up Michael
        consumed by *radical insufficiency*
    can't stop can't let go

his world sliding away
        in drugs laziness alienation
    we read in the papers

a month later he'd been busted
        for stealing a car in Florida
    what the fuck Florida

—he said he was gonna study
        —Florida god damn
    what a shame but

    Dale made it
        Billy made it
        Tinnin-Bey made it

    Robert needs a letter of recommendation
        for a counseling gig in Gary
    workin' with juvies
        he'll be perfect
          they'll love him

    Rice getting married in May
        saw Gary in the libes Tuesday
    postcards from Memphis

letters from Chicago
        collect calls from New York
    T. in grad school

living proof of the cruel error
                of *Body Count* creating
        Super-predators impulsive

        brutally remorseless they murder
        assault rape rob burglarize
        deal deadly drugs
        join gun-toting gangs
        create serious communal

        disorders Mr. Bennett[23]
                Mr. DiIulio Mr. Walters
        manufacturers of hate

        celebrating plantation myths
                your manipulated "data"
        reprising eugenics slavery

        claiming my friends produce
                criminogenic communities
        are cursed by *moral poverty*

        proclaiming *a moral case*
                for the death penalty[24]
        like whippings brandings

boring the tongue
        with a redhot bodkin[25]
for blaspheming God

Sarah M. Grimké stunned
        I *saw a human head*
        stuck up on a high pole

a runaway slave
        had been shot there
his head severed

as a terror
    to deter slaves
from running away[26]

such punishments futile
    enraging the human will
the gift of empathy shot

by your racist fury
    give 'em books jobs
respect not jails

practice the simple
    mechanics of enabling
dignity hope citizenship

the emergence of consciousness
    not a mystery but *a dialogue*
an intense faith in humankind[27]

with Jon the teacher friend
    up at dawn Saturday running
the foot path along the White River

steaming ancient oaks glowing
    transcendent yellows oranges
reds poplars shimmering

in soft morning breezes
    You feelin' like 5 or 7?
Let's do 7 past fishermen

dogs skateboard paperboys
    a mother and daughter
gathering leaves in their arms

Mom mom look at this one!
    Yes that's lovely across town
around the empty stadium

past the field hockey grounds
         they're kickin' ass first in the conference
through the quad past administration

by Greek's pizza sprinting
         the final four blocks leaves crunching
in rhythm sun now climbing

above the pale blue horizon
         bacon from open windows
filling the neighborhood

with the smell of plenty
         back at Jon's coffee
in the bath no shower

fillin' that damn kettle
         with soapy water
dump it on my head

hit the road by 8:00
         back to the prison
for Persuasion at 9:00

good food good music good run
         energized cleansed healed
with Jon's help realizing

being-in-the-world
         so clean simple
radical a critique

of insufficiency offered
         to me obliged now
to reciprocate I am

glad to be there
            overcome with joy
       almost weeping with

hitherto unknown compassion[28]
       saying *Good morning*
       gentlemen let's begin again

let's begin again

PROCLAMATION!

BY

THE GOVERNOR.

WHEREAS, an armed and organized body of the citizens of San Francisco County, has, in defiance of the Constitution and Laws of this State, assumed to exercise the powers of the Courts of Criminal Jurisdiction, and to pass and carry into effect extra-judicial sentences of death—and whereas a spirit of opposition to the Officers of the Law, while engaged in the execution of their duty, has been openly and publicly manifested; and there is reason to believe that further attempts may be made to interfere with the regular administration of justice in said County; and especially to take from the custody of the Sheriff certain Prisoners now confined in the Gaol of said County:

Now therefore, I, JOHN McDOUGAL, Governor of the State of California, do hereby call upon all good citizens of said County to unite for the purpose of sustaining public law and tranquillity, to aid the public officers in the discharge of their duty, and by all lawful means to discountenance any and every attempt which may be made to substitute the despotic control of a self-constituted association unknown and acting in defiance of the laws, in the place of the regularly organized government of the County. And I hereby call upon all public officers to be active, vigilant, and faithful in the performance of their trusts, and to resist to the utmost of their power, all efforts which may be made to subvert the laws and trample on the Constitution.

And I hereby warn those who are disposed to resist the legal authorities, that they cannot do so, without involving the community of which they are members in all the horrors of Civil War, subjecting life, liberty and property to the most fearful sacrifices.

The Government is determined, at all hazards, to sustain the Constitution and Laws, public peace can only be secured, and public liberty can only be maintained, by a strict adherence to that feeling of subordination to the law, and respect for its ministers, which have heretofore characterized the American People.

The attention of all citizens is requested to Sections 36 to 50, of "An Act to regulate proceedings in Criminal cases."

It is earnestly hoped that no necessity will arise calling for the execution of those provisions, and that the good sense and calm reflection of all good citizens will induce them to refrain from committing any acts calculated to destroy the peace and order of the community, and to bring the authorities into conflict with any portion of the People.

JNO. McDOUGAL,

Governor of California.

San Francisco, August 20th, 1851.

"DO RIGHT AND FEAR NOT!":
FIVE MEDITATIONS ON SAN QUENTIN

For Jody Lewen, Sean McPhetridge, and my students in San Quentin

I. *Pronounced Kaynteen*

The Richmond Bridge bends
        gently across the Bay
    double-tiered street lamps

fluorescent warning beacons
        blinking through fog
    entwined with brake lights

triangular streams of highbeams
        carving mathematical swaths
    of blindness illuminating

elegant arcs of concrete
        rain-soaked gleaming
    in the slow pulsing colors

of roller-coasters Ferris
        wheels the enchanting
    technology of forgetting

spotted with battered cars
        of lonely wives angry children
    the Visitor Parking Lot empties

down to the water lapping
        oil-smudged sand
    as supertankers glide

through the swirling haze
        mere outlines hinting
    at discharge gathering

in clumps along the shoreline
        where sheaths of eucalyptus
    bark and fallen needles

gather in smelly
        tarred-and-feathered
    pin-cushions

    the Franciscan Fathers
            first ventured here
        in the spring of 1817

    canoeing down the San Rafael
            Creek winding through dense
        Blackberry tangles clustered

    along *the flat stretch
        of pickleweed marsh*[1]
    where the Miwoks lived

    according to seasons
            beyond time until
        Quintun *pronounced Kaynteen*[2]

    gathered his men for battle
            against Mexican soldiers
        firing metal from giant rifles

    ripping bodies in half
            mysterious explosions
        launched into camp

from floating cities of fire
        yet the conquerors in such awe
of Quintun's valor in death

they willed to history his memory
        as *Rancho Punta de Quintun*
only to have Americans

*thinking all Spanish places
        were prefaced with "San"*[3]
rename the land San Quentin

II. *Rhythmic Secrets*

Walking to class across
        the late April courtyard
Pacific sun sliding

behind Mount Tamalpais
        back-lighting clusters of roses
enflaming *sun-stricken gun-towers*

*while gulls wheel above
        their shrill plaintive cries*[4]
showering gardenias shadowed by

palm trees ringing Memorial Circle's
        tombstones honoring officers
lost in the course of duty

facing the stuccoed Chapel
        where Friars walk in pairs
full-bodied brown wool

robes performing the dignity
        of penitent self-denial
and the folly of forgetting

Eco's simple confession
   I have come to believe
the whole world is

a harmless enigma
      made terrible by
our own mad attempt

to interpret it
      as though it had
an underlying truth[5]

the evening choir swells
      into *rhythmic secrets*
filling the evening

with harmonic promises
      waves of voices raised
to praise forgiveness

the ear perceives
      more than can
be explained for

joy is always a paradox[6]

III. *Tired of the Law*

Glorious recently stolen
   California is a Garden of
Eden besotted with gold[7]

wheat gold fruit gold
      drunken speculating thugs
refusing to pay taxes

the most desperate scoundrels
        accomplished in every act of
villainy became a State[8]

on 9 September 1850
        the 49ers *had come*
to acquire wealth

not to build institutions
        or participate in democratic
exercises their shanty towns[9]

rocked with treachery
        greed ambition desperate
men their wives left

at home no check
        upon appetites desires
devouring gluttony

        the *absolution from social duties*
                capitalism's gift to the frontier
        the struggle for wealth

        so fierce *communities rotted*
                till rottenness could no longer
        be endured the strong[10]

        gathering their friends
                neighbors debtors together
        enacting justice

        the frontier way
                quickly brutally
        without trial

        soon the Sierras crusted
                with the blood of strangers
        men chosen for their weakness

their accent their preference
      for corn tortillas
   over flour bread

the killings done
      in the name of democracy
   no lawyers to delay

no petty technicalities[11]
      just men with guns
   and ropes and bibles

San Francisco soon sliding
      into gold and whiskey-
   induced chaos uproar

violence *so much*
      was hopelessly crooked
   sordid mean[12]

   homesick Milo Goss
      writes to his mother
   back in Michigan

San Francisco is wickedness
      in its worst forms
   vice in disgusting forms[13]

   fires of dubious origin
      consume the wooden city
   The Alta selling fear

there is an organized band
      villains determined to
   destroy this city[14]

after a crime on 19 February
      1851 Sam Brannan shouts
   to his fellow citizens

frustrated hysterical
  I am tired of the law![15]
hanging is in the air

The Courier shrieking
  the first law of nature demands
criminals be *instantly shot*

hung burned alive[16]
  otherwise *there is no security*
for life and property[17]

the founding fathers agree
  their Committee of Vigilance
a gentlemen's lynching club

founded June 8th 1851
  their constitution railing
against *the quibbles of the law*

the insecurity of prisons
  the corruption of the police
those who pretend

to administer justice[18]
  citizens of property rallying
the Ladies of the Trinity Parish

celebrate righteous fury
  by sewing a silk banner
Do Right and Fear Not![19]

three days later Jenkins
  a common ruffian
is escorted by *the best*

known men of the city[20]
  to a hasty gallows
drunken crowds cheering

the spectacle of *cross-roads justice*[21]
    the old fashioned way
the Committee emboldened

arrests 91 *thieves burglars*
    incendiary assassins gamblers
disturbers of the peace

14 ordered to leave California
14 deported from America
41 discharged
    15 handed to authorities
    2 undesignated
    1 whipped
    4 hanged[22]

the mob running rampant
    Governor McDougal aghast
plasters the town with posters

calling for restraint
    all good citizens unite
sustain public law

do not fall for the romance of
    despotic associations defying the laws[23]
we must have strict adherence

to the law soon persuading
    hungover vigilantes
that law and order might be

administered more efficiently
    by policemen prisons
the bureaucrats' dignified

masquerade of modern justice
    than by thundering clouds
of dust on drunken nights

filled with torchlit rumors

IV. *Selling Cheap*

With no money no law
        no prison no Capitol
    los jefes James Madison Estell

y Mariano Guadalupe Vallejo
        propose a deal the penniless
    infant state can not refuse

a plum parcel of their land
        plus $125,000 in cash
    for a new capitol building

in exchange for a ten-year lease
        on the state's convict labor
    established as landlords

the state's new captains of peonage
        on April 25 1851 Estell *y* Vallejo
    moor their floating prison

off Angel Island the *Waban*
        a 268 ton merchant vessel
    shorn of its masts

bought by former Texas Ranger
        turned Sheriff Jack Hayes
    17 of the first 34 prisoners escaped[24]

celebrating Bastille Day
        14 July 1852
    former-Governor McDougal and Estell

sail their musty kingdom North
>with drink and song and prostitutes
>draped in bunting honoring

>>*Liberté*
>>>*Égalité*
>>>>*Fraternité*

grounding their investment
>at Point San Quentin
>greeting Thomas Johns the Know Nothing

entrepreneur scoundrel
>happily building America's Bastille
>on a poison oak covered 20-acre plot

secured from Benjamin Buckalew
>with $10,000 of the state's money
>*that land was not worth $5 an acre*[25]

the surrounding 16 acres
>traded by Buckalew to Estell
>for $5 *a gift* to launch

The San Francisco Manufacturing Company[26]
>making bricks with prison labor
>for "The Stones" the first prison

building contracted to
>the Know Nothing Johns
>for $135,000 in a no-bid

gentleman's deal *suspicion*
>*great that bribery accounted* [27]
>for the cozy enriching

of self and friends
>citizens soon calling it
>*the state prison swindle*[28]

Estell reminds the doubtful
        that corrupt prisons are
    better than the thuggery

of those who *run down*
        tether and strangle
    a few poor affrighted wretches[29]

he avoids prison conflict
        by selling "escapes"
    for as much as $200

some 87 in 1854 alone
        the year of escapes[30]
    or by flogging laggards

who refuse to make bricks
        ten lashes or by "showering"
    men *tied upside down naked* [31]

with second-hand gold-mining jets
        hydraulic streams of freezing water
    so powerful they stripped the Sierra

foothills filling the Yuba River
        with deadly tailings *it would*
    cut a man in two it if hit him[32]

but the best money ventures
        were smuggling drink opium women
    to those who could not purchase freedom

    all manner of illicit trade[33]
        enriching Estell
    but none as satisfying

as selling niggers
        to pirate slave-dealers
    up from New Orleans[34]

V. *The Dignity of Baseball*

We sit in a circle discussing Cesare Beccaria's *On Crimes and Punish-ments*. Written in 1764, it is both a passionate argument for judicial pru-dence and the first significant anti-death penalty treatise of the Enlight-enment. Outside our windows, the prison all-star baseball team drubs some local club. Rumor suggests it is the Policeman's Benevolence As-sociation team, making the thrashing doubly edifying. At break time we line the windows, arms dangling into the sweet evening air:

> *Freako played for State, woulda' been drafted—*
>> *No way; can't hit for power—*
>>> *Better'n Bogues's range; better'n Smitty's speed—*

> *So Beccaria printed this in secret? Hiding in his basement?*
>> *I heard they was scoutin' him the night he went down.*
>>> *But you said Bentham loved him—*

> *No way—*
>> *I'm tellin' you, man.*
>>> *Isn't that where Foucault cops the panopticon stuff?*

> *No way—*
>> *That's bullshit. He playin' you—*
>>> *Yeah, and Linebaugh talks about his working in the ship-yards, for the Czar—or was that his brother, Samuel?*

> *I'm tellin' you. His sister, man, she knows.*[35]

The recreation yard sits next to and below the education building. Our windows look onto the banks of lights towering over the field, our view partially blocked by tangled masses of heating pipes and steel bars. The roar of the fans lofts up through the crisp tangy air, settling down on our discussion, the men grinning with each eruption of applause, chuck-ling with every crack of the bat.

As the Bay wind changes direction we hear the slightest trace of the choir's *rhythmic secrets* floating across the yard just as another monster

smash rockets through the glare of the lights, parting a sea of bugs danc-
ing around the towers

          before disappearing
             into the sweet darkness
          of another brilliant

          San Quentin evening

PERHAPS SOME GRACE

For Michael Staneck, Erica Thompson, and my students
in the Indiana Correctional Facility

I. *Not an Anomaly*

    through fogged charter bus windows
        and wary talk of choke-holds
    we roll down Indiana State Road 41

    urban messengers bearing
        the underclass's rage
    not an anomaly

    but an expected outcome
        logical perhaps even
    the *necessary* by-product

    of the undeniable laws
        of American capitalism as
    conditioned by white supremacy[1]

    to obscure rural hell-holes
        the new supermax prison
    at Wabash Valley[2]

    where spring streams crest
        over drainage ditches sweeping
    trailer parks off cinder blocks

in waves of spontaneous mud
        plowing dung and seed and
    balled up McDonalds wrappers

across swampy black fields
        storming southward to Vincennes
    the Wabash eventually draining

into the coal-barge-infested
        Ohio River sliding west
    onward to the Mississippi

    a grocery bag of left-over
        pro bono bagels
    clambers from seat to seat

    strangers tapping shoulders
        of comrades-for-the-day
    offering sweet sustenance

to their fellow abolitionists
        as we compare notes
    on slanted media coverage

    recalling Marcuse's prophesy
        the mobilization of all media
    for the defense of the established

    reality has coordinated the means
        of expression to the point
    communication is *impossible*[3]

while fidgeting atop *The Nation*
        crumpled between pillows
    and stacks of chant sheets

where terror madness evil
        are reduced to nursery rhymes
    we chant in embarrassment

Hey hey, ho ho, state torture has got to go!
Hey hey, ho ho, to supermaxes we say no!

Governor Bayh, we ask why?
Why do you sponsor genocide?

rumbling sleepily southward
  through the littered wreckage
poking holes for arms and heads

in jumbo green glad-bags
  suburban-lawn-care-size
the forethought of a lifetime

organizer covering for
  revolutionaries too obsessed
with smashing the state

to pack an umbrella
  for a road trip
in monsoon season

  Nancy gathered the bills
    crazy Abby and the boys
  rained down on Wall St. in '72

  Michael did two honorable years
    in a federal pen for picnicking
  on an MX silo in the Dakotas

  Tinnin-Bey paid fourteen years
    growing wiser older sadder
  for a crime he didn't commit

  Stan simmers in his mumbling
    psychotic rage from a lifetime
  of lost loony causes

Rosalie passes around faded
        photos of nationalist 'rades
held in solitary confinement

    for the *seditious conspiracy*
        of fighting *U.S. imperialism*
    rationalized by a *legal system*

    that has been the instrument
        to impose tyranny demanding
    Fourth-World Liberation[4]

Hondo plans the second secession
    of Florida Georgia Alabama South Carolina
Dixie rising as the return of the repressed

to form the reparations land-grant
    Revolutionary Afrikan People's Republic
blithe and secure confidently ignorant

of the encumbrances of history
    and the deep politics of weapons Disney
Coca-Cola petrochemical sweetheart deals

    we are a traveling circus
        of fringe elements freaks
    malcontents would-be *Jacobins*

    too smart for the nightly dose
        of State propaganda
    but too stupid to find solace

    in the numbed netherworld
        of consumer communities
    instead struggling for equality

        not just freedom
            the license to consume
        destroy forget

but something greater
        than rationalized complicity
with callousness so common

now inseparable from breathing

II. *Gene Debs's Hometown*

The Supermax lies half-buried
        an impregnable bunker of misery
embitterment humiliation

27 sorry miles south
        of Gene Debs's hometown
once-thriving Terre Haute

one of ten children
        Gene worked the rail yards
attacking *corporation lawyers*

cowardly politicians
        the tyranny of phony patriotism
money's lure to war

preaching *I would rather be*
        a thousand times a free soul in jail
than a sycophant and coward on the street

landed Gene in the slammer
        for thumbing his nose
at Mr. Wilson's Espionage Acts[5]

the Feds sent Gene to Atlanta
        where he was serenaded to sleep
by supporters outside the prison

so Gene ran for president from his cell
   asking the workers of the world to vote
  For President, Convict No. 9653

 The Lincoln of the Wabash was lucky[6]
   today he'd be sent
  to a supermax

of perpetual solitary confinement
   24-hour lights on never night
  no windows no watches allowed

a timeless pit of torture
   physical psychological spiritual
  officially cloaked violence[7]

a *Hell Factory* decorated[8]
   by doubled rows of razor wire
  a phalanx of motion sensors

search-light sharp-shooter towers
   ringing a compound plantation
  housing *Slaves of the State*[9]

 no longer forced producers
   now forced consumers
  the nation's fastest growing

 food market devouring goods
   over $1 billion per year[10]
  a Campbell's Soup official

chuckling anonymously
   The more crooks you have
  the better business is for us[11]

 guards watch from air-conditioned booths
   videotaping our chants and testimonies
  for their drunken entertainment

at the year-end awards ceremony
    where best marksman angler
   and most "cell extraction" takedowns

like the guards in Westville's MCC
    Maximum Control Complex
   Indiana's supermax prison

for "the worst of the worst"
    where guards *beat senseless*
   Aaron Isby while shackled

by hands feet waist genitals
    immobilized in iron chains
   then stripped him naked

tied face-down spread-eagle
    to a metal bed frame
   left for days in feces

forced to wear a hockey mask
    the prison superintendent
   claiming Isby's allegations

are totally without truth
    the DOC took *appropriate steps*
   to handle the situation[12]

all win NRA jackets high fives
    a month of free shots
   at Todd's raceway lounge

and though our tax dollars
    have paid for every square
   inch of concrete *$351 billion*

over the next ten years[13]
        we are denied access
        to the prison parking lot

    troopers lead us instead
                to the soupy shoulder
        where nuns mothers children

    disembark into muddy puddles
                as banners posters pickets
        leap into angry hands

                Education not torture!
                        Que salgan ya! Que salgan ya!
                No Peace without Justice!

    the Maoists from St. Louis
                four hours southwest
        pass out fliers against gentrification

    the Anarchists from Ft. Wayne
                four hours northeast
        lecture the police on strip searches

    our signs are ripped to shreds
                in the stinging horizontal rain
        leaving us tattered drenched

    ankle deep in cold mud
                knee deep in wispy prairie grass
        pathetic comic enraged

        the local TV station has sent
                a twenty-three year old intern
        bleached-blonde reporter

        she arrives in heels makeup streaking
                disbelieving happily unaware
        that Amnesty International

and Human Rights Watch
      decry supermaxes
   as human rights violations[14]

as systematic torture so cruel
      Jerome Miller suggests
   their wardens have become

worthy of shameful comparison
      to *Nuremberg's celebrated*
war criminals[15]

she asks smart questions
      and receives pages of statistics
   horror stories from ex-prisoners

coffee stained photographs
      from mothers begging for mercy
   from wives hoping for justice

from children crying for love
      anger from revolutionaries
   shouting dogmas from Freddy

and crazy Ramona Afrika
      to a white country girl
   who has never ventured

across state lines
      or felt the sadness
   of a world swirling beyond

the fraternal Autumnal cheer
      of the annual I.U./Purdue
   Old Oaken Bucket Game

the highway slowly clogs
      with afternoon shoppers
   entranced by Walmart's wonders

slowing for a quick peek
>> at the splattered fanatics
> marching in circles

through the swamp-land
>> repeating stupid chants
> into the slicing wind

dwarfed by thunder
>> State Trooper sirens
> and impromptu gifts

of southern kindness
>> offered from pick-ups
> and duct-taped Fords

> *Get a job asshole!*
>> *They wouldn't be here*
>>> *if they hadn't asked for it!*
>> *Niggers go home!*

and I imagine old Gene
>> gliding ghostly overhead
> wagging his *insistent finger*

You need to know
>> *that you are fit for something better*
> *than slavery and cannon fodder*[16]

III. *The Nausea*

I remember a bitter Winter
>> afternoon in February 1996
> dappled slate gray sky

lording existential emptiness
>> above all hope howling
> prairie wind ripping

through hats jackets gloves
        merciless even the guard
    dogs shiver in their huts

too cold to sniff for contraband
        as the evening chow lines
    shuffle across the yard

IV. *Julius Don't Wear No Socks*

Groups of men erupt
        through bullet-proof doors
    stomping off snow

hanging identical numbered jackets
        on identical numbered chairs
    dumping out dog-eared essays

packets of zu-zus and wham-whams
        transforming from offenders
    to college students

God damn it's cold; hey man, wuz up?
    Hey Stephen, bro, how's the drive in this weather?
Anybody seen a stapler?
    Haug's crazy man, that's all I gotta' say—what kinda'
writin' is that?
    East German Marxists all write like that—it's the
bureaucracy. . .

anxious to tackle Haug's *Commodity*
        Aesthetics, Ideology, and Culture[17]
    we pull our chairs together

a huddled team of scholars addicts
        fathers could'a-beens lost souls
    struggling for enlightenment

redemption some minor epiphany
       perhaps some grace
  to carry us to the 7:30 count

hollered by guards in the hallway
       bored annoyed smirking
  at our joyous conversation

    Julius sits across the circle
           in faded jeans gray
      prison-issue sweatshirt

   ID number stamped
         across his breast
     birthday present sneakers

squishing softly
       in a muddy puddle
  of melted snow

    Julius, no socks?
         It's ten below and snowy
      and you're stylin' with no socks?

    Burke looks up from his notes
         Julius' cheerful bunkee
      battered wool skull cap

   drooping to one side
         pen dangling
     from his laconic smile

    Julius don't wear no socks

   the son of an immigrant
         Bengali neuro-surgeon
     looks up amused annoyed

Why bother?
          you're outta here after class
     off for dinner with friends

part 'a the world
          meeting people you love
     I'm back in G-house

with dumbo and sneezey
          one more down and
     fifteen-hundred and seventy-two

more to go What do I care
          how I look? How I feel?
     I have no one I care to impress

They can have my body
          it's theirs they own it
     and control it they tell me

when to sleep they tell me
          when to piss they tell me
     when to eat

so socks are irrelevant
          The mind is all that's left
     and all that matters

spirit genius imagination
          transcendence
     the physical man shit

     I left that behind years ago
          as Julius speaks
     I hear the sweet echo

     of Judee Norton swearing
          I am captured
     but not subdued

> *they think they have me*
> > *but my mind wheels and soars*
> *no prisoner*
>
> *I am free*[18]

V. *Tired Hope*

So we tromp through the grass
> cold mud oozing into boots
encasing calves in gluey pants

plastered to itchy skin our
> hands passing from stinging
pain to frozen numbness

our voices gone hoarse
> from hurling possibilities
at the death machine's

lackeys and yes-men
> while the sleep-walking
masses drone by

honking horns of terror
> drowning out all hope
with their tribal hatred

> *impenetrable meaningless*
> > *the anger against all*
> *that is different*[19]

so we march through the mud
> exercising the last vestiges
of what was once citizenship

in a democracy
>   long since exchanged
> for shopping malls

manufacturer's outlets
>   food courts free appetizers
> *Labor Day Specials!*

> hoping against all hope
>>   to create a story
>> a song a friendship

> something we can laugh about
>>   while shivering our way home
>> before emptying back

> into lonely cars
>>   and quiet apartments
>> where the only thing

>>   worse than lost causes
>>>   is the quiet creeping terror
>>> of learned indifference

>>   thrilled exhausted satisfied
>>>   to have spoken acted moved
>>> I drive home along Clark

>>   the young man stops
>>>   offers a gentle hand
>>> walks the old woman

>>   across the bustling street
>>>   the light turns green
>>> they're in the crosswalk

>>   no one honks no one
>>>   moves no one shouts
>>> we see the kindness

we wait for the gift
        to complete its course
they make their corner

she turns to him thankful
        he nods she nods I nod
the world redeemed

for a moment a flash
        a second long enough
to honor hope dignity

        perhaps some grace

Emptiness Doesn't Take Notice: Supermax Poems

For Seth Donnelly, the *Human Rights Held Hostage* community,
and The Committee to End the Marion Lockdown[1]

I. *The Tour*

Scrubbed white hallways aerodynamic
        rotating lights lowering mysteriously
    from seamless recesses policing

our halting conversation erupting
        in deafening blinding disorienting
    terror *Offender out of cell Offender*

out of cell signaling free citizens
        to scurry for cover nearest door
    protected zone hidden from *Offender*

out of cell young man head shaven yellow
        jump suit cotton slippers no socks
    hands shackled together by chains

looped 'round neck waist feet rope
        taught against genitals trailing
    behind between legs *that's the tail*

        held by a guard guarded
          by a guard guarded
            by a guard

if he runs
yank the tail
down he goes

we duck into the guard's equipment room
        batons riot shields boots shin pads
    hanging in a row like Sears JCPenney

a tailor's rack of flack jackets helmets
        rifles shotguns pistols cuffs
    arms against *the baddest of the bad*[2]

Mr. Bennett's *Super Predators*[3]
        chains looped 'round neck
    waist feet my most enduring

memory producing *ontological vomiting*[4]
        rows of thick black shin pads
    catcher's gear for Little League Baseball

hanging neatly treated with respect
        tools well-used scratched chipped
    cut chunks missing the traces

of another stomping cell-extraction
        every shin pad met
    by a face an arm an ankle

each mark a testimony to terror
        meant to drive you insane
    the deprivation of one's humanity

produces *severe paranoia*
            your impulse control starts to go
    you become mad[5]

like Charlie Chase in Massachusetts
        a sick kid made sicker by isolation
    beatings self-mutilations left to rot

to kill himself to simmer in a stew
     of *Depakene Tegretol Thorazine Navane*
Zoloft Klonopin Trazadone Inderal[6]

my other enduring memory
     the control booth circular
   glass walls automated surveying

double tiers ringing the bunker
     flashing meters knobs levers
   like television technical inhuman

no one moves without
     clearance no one moves
   without guards no one

moves without hands
     shackled chains looped
   'round neck waist feet

each passage monitored
     each window reinforced
   each guard armed

   all furniture is unmovable
   no soap dish no knobs no
   toilet seats no toilet handles
   all potential weapons

security so tight at Florence
     they built six guard towers
   to thwart air attack[7]

impossible to escape
     yet above me
   a frayed rope

dangling from the ceiling
       little plastic ring tied to the end
what's this? I ask

Oh you never know
       says my guide
yanking the rope

down pops a folded stairway
       like the one leading to
Grandma's musty old attic

opening mercifully
       onto the dreamy blue
autumnal Indiana sky

II. *Evan's Face*

Everybody was high-fiving
       shaking hands
congratulating each other

bragging about
       how much butt
you kicked

so says Tactical Squad Lieutenant Ray McWhorter
regarding the *celebratory chicken dinner*
following the 10 July 1996 Hays State Prison mauling[8]

Georgia prison guards
       cheered on by D.O.C.
Commissioner Wayne Garner

beat naked prisoners
       hands shackled to chains
looped 'round neck waist

feet smashing their faces
        into concrete walls
    you know that sound

the dull hollow thud
        of a skull cracking
    like a pumpkin

split open sticky orange
        seeds membranes spilling
    across the Halloween floor

it kind of splattered out
        in like a circular pattern
    dripping down the wall[9]

    like Evan the goalie
            outstretched diving
        left hand deflecting

    the whistling shot
            we're leaping *yes yes*
    high-fiving *great save*

    Evan's face smashes
            the goal-post cracking
    nose cheek jaw teeth

    flying blood pooling
            in the Autumn mud
    his face gone

    erased just pulp
            Chris crawling
    through the mud

    gathering teeth
            Danny throwing up
    others back away

stunned into silence
        mesmerized by
    their first sight

of the inside of a head
        intricate pink throbbing
    overwhelmed be fear

my only thought to run
        for help the nearest house
    safe zone Ficks Colavitas

phone please somebody
        quick please somebody
    he's gonna die stomach

churning vision blurred
        incomprehensible disgust
    the body so fragile broken

painful Evan writhing
        in the grass eyes wide
    hands holding his brain

spitting teeth dirt blood
        between screams
    that childhood field haunted

by the dull thud of flesh
        echoing through the trees
    Evan lived he played again

a folk hero *jeez what a save*
        gave his body for the team
    it's not death I fear

but pain the unspeakable
        complicity of knowing
    somewhere a guard

high-fives his buddies
                after crushing
        another face

into another wall
                in another prison
        where another life

splatters out
                in a circular pattern
        dripping down the wall

III. *The Gladiators*

I came from a cadre of about twenty-five percent of the Correctional
Peace Officers that are Vietnam veterans, and I think the real reason
we stayed on is because of the abnormal amount of agent orange
that we absorbed.

Perhaps that explains it
        Mr. Don Novey
        President of CCPOA[10]

the most powerful union
        in California greasing
        the wheels of Governor

Pete Wilson and lackey
        Attorney General Dan
        Lungren's holy crusade

against the underclass
        The Chronicle calling it
        a reign of death[11]

shelling out *$1 million since 1990*
        $5.2 million to candidates since 1987
        $760,000 in 1990 alone

to target Diane Feinstein[12]
  that bitch feminist
 soft on crime

 we need men like Pio Cruz
   the CCPOA union rep.
  Corcoran guard

ring announcer
  and gunner
 for the gladiator cockfights[13]

  43 wounded 7 killed
    between 1989 and 1995
  175 wounded 27 killed

  statewide *between '89 and '94*
    yet *only one man armed*
 with a weapon when shot[14]

Corcoran a $272 million brutality
  factory in 1988 its first year open
 1500 fights 662 firings of 37 mm gas guns

launching wood blocks at men fighting
  for the guards' gambling pleasures
 47 discharges of 9 mm assault rifles[15]

 twelve prisons in California in 1984
   twenty-one built since then
  DOC budget *$3.9 billion per year*

 charging *$26,690 per prisoner*
  over *160,000* prisoners
 48,756 employees

 staffing *33 state prisons*
   38 camps in wilderness areas
  16 community correctional facilities[16]

confirming Christie's awful thesis
With a view on crime
as an unlimited natural resource

for the crime control industry
The economic interests
of the industry will always be

on the oversupply
of police and prisons
thus *establishing*

an extraordinarily strong
force for the expansion
of the system[17]

lawsuits brought forward yet
the Wilson Administration
blocked all *efforts*

to investigate brutality[18]
appointing instead
Del Pierce *Mr. Fix It*[19]

to oversee the DOC team
It was just a sham
says Jim Connor[20]

supervisor of the investigation
the final DOC report
a whitewash a favor

State Senator Hayden
appalled calling it
a tremendous sanitizing[21]

we know the CCPOA
ordered guards not to speak
more than 90 Corcoran officers

marched in and out
    of fact-finding *interviews*
without answering

a single question[22]
    with the blessing
of Warden *Mushroom*

George Smith *he likes*
    to be kept in the dark[23]
hiding behind Rawls'

unfortunate suggestion
    a veil of ignorance
levels commitments

equalizes *assets* and *abilities*
    intelligence strength and the like[24]
instead a bureaucrat's dream

my hands are clean
    I didn't know
wasn't aware

impossible preposterous
    how could you not know
"The Sharks" greeting

busloads of new prisoners
    with the guard cheer
Welcome to Hell![25]

36 black prisoners
    from Calipatria beaten
21 June 1995

as they left the bus
    shackled for transfer
six men with broken ribs[26]

the rest reminded
       socialized again
into a living *Hell*

governed by blood
       cheap and plentiful
and men who cheer

as it *splatters out*
       in a circular pattern
    dripping down the wall

IV. *Historical Vengeance*

David Walker pled 170 years ago
    See your Declaration Americans!!
  Do you understand your own language?[27]

slavery so base immoral profitable
    like the wondrously expensive
technology of supermaxes

teaching even *decent men*
    to regard killing their fellows
as one of their duties[28]

Walker writing from Boston
    smuggling his tracts South
sewn into second-hand trousers

a lone voice bleeding in the trees
    sneaking amidst whips chains dogs
years before Grimké Weld Child

confronting a monolith
    a culture of death
committed to white supremacy

since Columbus captured the first slaves
in a 1495 raid on Hispaniola
where he *slaughtered 250,000 Arawaks*

sending the 500 *best specimens*
back to Spain proclaiming
in the name of the Holy Trinity

let us send
    all the slaves
that can be sold[29]

the modernizing British
            entrepreneurial excited
by cheap labor

imperial expansion *their errand*
            into Africa was not
a new or a perfect community

but a business trip
        with no hope
for civilizing the Negro's

steaming continent[30]
            the unhappy wretches
then diagnosed by

doctor gentleman slavemaster
            Samuel Cartwright
as suffering *a disease*

of the mind causing
        them to run away
he called it *Drapetomania*[31]

not unlike Mr. Bennett's
        superpredators who suffer
from moral poverty

the virtual absence
        of people who teach morality[32]
like your friends

Hernstein and Murray's
        Bell Curve where
Mr. Francis Galton

the godfather of eugenics
        stalks the pages
        scalpel in hand

He was on the right track
        after all they gush[33]
echoing your plea

for *a moral case for*
        the death penalty[34]
of course of course

why not kill them all
        the niggers the Jews
the spicks the Irish

like Mr. Robert Buchanan
        reporting in 1824
        to his fellow phrenologists

that James Gordon's hanging
        was necessary fair just
        for he was *Roman Catholic*

repulsive deplorably ignorant
        idle inefficient small witted
possessed by *brutal ferocity*

and *barbarous methods* Mr. Buchanan[35]
        have you any evidence
        the man is guilty?

The Boston Prison Discipline Society
your peers so convinced
blacks and Irish cause crime

they announce in 1826
the first cause of the increase
in crime is the degraded

character of the coloreds[36]
now we call it intelligence testing
IQ SAT CAT supermax

criminogenic Superpredator
the new vocabulary of slavery
in the face of this monstrosity

Mr. Walker challenged
the most skilled historians
to show me

a parallel of barbarity
show me
the parallel of cruelties

in the annals
of heathens or devils[37]
Mr. Walker I see

not parallels
but continuities
our nation blinded

by fear prejudice
anger embodying
Rousseau's charge

honor without virtue
reason without wisdom
pleasure without happiness[38]

Transcending Schelling's Lament

For B.A.K.

The infinite possibilities
      of good and evil jostle
   as *a bond of freedom*

one *cannot remain*
      in indecision for God
   must necessarily reveal

Himself through our actions
      but we are weak afraid
   jealous unworthy instead

choosing *false pleasures*
      the hunger of selfishness
   ravenous poisonous[1]

leaving God jilted
      rebuffed squandering
   our imposed freedom

on banality decadence
      God unhappy devising
   our punishment to walk

forever haunted by
      the veil of sadness
   spread over all nature

the deep unappeasable
         melancholy of all life
     Joy must have sorrow

Sorrow must be
         transfigured in joy[2]
     settled slowly down

     around me noon last
             Wednesday Hertz Hall
         elegant paneled wood

     shimmering utopian Berkeley
             reflected through stained
         glass seven octave fairy tale

         pipe organ Easter in Chartres
                 peasants leave their sheep
             in the misty gray courtyard

     Latin mass swirling
             incense dripping ceiling
         organ booming waves of

     sound shaking ancient pews
             deafening like a kick drum
         but louder scarier enveloping

     all sensations consciousness
             in God's secret harmonies
         rhythms layered promises

         I wish I believed I wish
                 I could forget Tom Paine's
             scorching prison treatise

the French scared
       by Britain's 1793 invasion
    tossing the author of their

constitution in the slammer
       just four years after
    the revolution torched

with his words the old order
       the aristocracy the dead world
    embodied in the church

set up to terrify and enslave
       Paine barking from jail
    against *the idolatry of*

the ancient mythologies calling
       for *The Age of Reason*
    it is only by the exercise

of reason that man can
       discover God Mr. Schelling[3]
    appalled Hegel Novalis

    Goethe all abandoning
       the primal Being matter[4]
    for the mechanistic

    intuitionist imperial
       disgusted Schelling losing
    a friend a day bickering

    amidst *a literary salon*
       scattered over the whole
    of Germany feuding

through *the anarchy of*
living while worshipping
the new truths new sciences

their heroically frivolous
flight towards heaven[5]
blinding them forgetting

one can not
through pure reason
become virtuous[6]

I'd settle for a blanket
my panniers drenched
from weeks of rain

I love Paris in the springtime[7]
no way my ass
driven here for warmth

dry ground still I
wish I believed I wish
I could believe in

God's grace inhabiting
the organ towering
above a packed house

students professors friends
lovers I wonder if
we'll become *how*

do we know we are
not already somebody's
tomorrow? between songs[8]

whispering cheek to cheek
    your hair brushing my
  shoulder elbows touch

        I'm fifteen walking
            to school *Remember*
        the Maine! cutting

        through the morning
            woods dewy grass
        clumping to my Keds

        new orange laces
            so cool so cool so cool
        I hoped but now

        my feet cold shivering
            not yet aware of
        this diversion of aim

        beginning the sublimation
            of sexual instincts still[9]
        driven possessed magical

        prismatic light filtered
            through oaks birches
        willows casting shadows

        across your face you
            slide in and out
        between dream and

        projection the sight
            of the beloved
        is the thing you love

most between songs[10]
        stealing glances beautiful
I am unraveled

into another condition[11]
        Red apple full of color
a little worm eats your core

love a thorn
        that punches the heart[12]
Sarajevo folk song blessed

with medieval recorders
        viola de gamba
guitars tambourines voices

all remembering lamenting
        five hundred years of exile
Sephardic Jews fleeing

Christian Imperial Spain
        the inquisition's genocidal
madness we sit in

silence seduced
        I see you in Morocco
Istanbul Jerusalem Berkeley

now half a millennium later
        still *love alone acts*
as the civilizing factor

through the focused
        energy of *instincts*
inhibited in their aims[13]

buried stifled perhaps
        channeled into poetry
the veil of sadness

at 1:00 sharp we part
        you to teach me
to teach in a daze

Forché's gentle genius
        her childhood friend
Victoria plotting escape

from dreary Michigan
        trailer parks to glory
uninhibited in Montréal

where a québeçoise could sing
        take any man's face
to her unfastened blouse

and wake to wine
        on the bedside table[14]
I whisper these lines

my students tremble in
        anticipation yes it's true
you can leave you can

get out you can
        love with abandon
yet even *the wine*

on the bedside
        cannot numb
the veil of sadness

Morrison's terrible lesson
  haunting the jumble
of unquenched desire

Violet searching the past
  digging through rubble
myth forgotten memories

imagining lost plenitude
  emptiness fulfillment
no it wasn't me he

wanted drawn instead
  to *things I should have*
known and didn't

secret things kept hidden
  who was it not me
at all who was he

thinking of me not
  me an image a dream
he had yet to see

but knew all about[15]
  but then naming our
mutual misrecognition

leads us slowly
  to accept the space
between us no longer

a problem a lacking
  just the inescapable
dilemma of imagination

memory projection
     the *veil of sadness*
giving way instead

to your teaching
     me to choose
love

ABOUT THE SAME AS COMMERCIAL FISHING

For Naneen Karraker, Christian Parenti, and Shawny Anderson

I. *The Dialectic of Perfection and Derangement*[1]

Red Bluff bakes slowly
　　　in the Northern cradle
　　of the Central Valley

circled by Lassen Peak's
　　　10,457' snowcap reflecting
　　piercing sunlight in the east

Mt. Shasta's 14,162' glaciers
　　　shimmering to the north
　　above deep emerald green

rice paddies flanking Route 99
　　　giving way to apricots
　　almonds olives grapes pears

bustling family farms with
　　　flags tractors fruit stands
　　where neighbors talk

　of the militias
　　　　gathering weapons
　　in the hills

we head out of town
          eastward on State Road 36
          toward Payne's Creek

a sleepy gathering
          of a dozen low houses
          one bar many horses

swishing flies amidst groves
          of gnarled oaks blackberries
          Little Giant Mill Road

winding through the foothills
          rusted truck in a field
          No Trespassing wired

to a cattle fence on Ponderosa Way
          winding up endless S-turns
          entering the Ishi Wilderness

          named after the Yahi Indians
          Ishi an *invaluable*
          Ethnographic source

          considered the last
          Stone Age survivor
          in the United States

dove-tailed into the sublime
          remnants of the forgotten
          great Pacific Ring of Fire

where Mount Tehama spewed
          rivers of lava clouds of ash
          melting all living things

600,000 years ago now[2]
> grown into our treasure
Lassen National Forest

seventeen meandering miles
> of rutted fire road
rattlers sunning on rocks

giant Ponderosa Sugar Pines
> canopied above the forest floor
Mill Creek crashing down

ravines waterfalls at every turn
> Bald Eagles glide overhead
sky pulsing in aching blue

cliffs rising hundreds of feet
> valleys disappearing into
shadows *I think we're lost*

what's that up ahead?
> *let's pull in they'll know*
—yes thank you officer

the cheerful Prison Camp Guard
> informs us the trailhead
is *just a bit further on*

II. *The Costume Party*

Going to jail is a gas
> a slumber-party for clerks
guards lawyers bureaucrats

donning striped uniforms
> party costumes loaned
by The March of Dimes

those *arrested* forced
            to make bail
        by leaning on

friends relatives and other
            staff to raise nearly $4,000
        photographed with grins

mock tough-guy poses
            in the *Correction News*
        beneath a happy story

about the *car washes*
            barbecues food sales
        that raised $14,000[3]

to throw a party for employees
            with 15 or more years of service
        in the CDC the largest colony

    prison plantation in America
            where *160,901 prisoners*
        celebrated the millennium

    where guards make *$44,000*
            per year and *pay $8 million*
        in dues to the CCPOA

    backing Three Strikes legislation
            calling for *21 new prisons*
        it will cost $40 billion[4]

    housing three-strike monsters
            like Anthony Garcia
        sentenced to *26 years to life*

for shoplifting
         several pairs
of pants[5]

    the costume party revelers
              not unlike Eichmann
         neither perverted nor sadistic

    just *terribly and terrifyingly*
         normal apparently
         impossible for him

    to know or to feel
              he was doing wrong
         he was not stupid

    it was sheer thoughtlessness
              can wreak more havoc
         than all the evil instincts[6]

    of Deputy Director of Administrative Services
              James Tilton
    former Chief Deputy Director of Field Operations
         Judge Eddie Meyers
    Special Assistant to the Deputy Director
              Louis DiNinni

who don't realize
         their funny costumes
    sentence their colleagues
              to death by boredom

the famous San Quentin uniforms
         instituted in 1865
    mark shorties with vertical stripes
              lifers with horizontal stripes[7]

III. *This is Mine*

> *The narcotic tobacco haze of capitalism*[8]
> *must have prison to protect itself*
> *from the criminals it has created*[9]

to keep the rabble in line
        your jewels safe
between 1916-1934

of the 26,669 prisoners at San Quentin
    16% committed robbery
        24% burglary
            18% theft and fraud
            14% forgery

    72% of all prisoners
        doing hard *time*
        for property crimes[10]

for succumbing to desire
        the logical result of capitalism
    coveting the fruits of their labor

they'd mined that gold
        sewn that shirt harvested
    that wheat laid that rail

    like John Ward an officer
        in the British raid on Senegal
    in 1758 *plunder valued*

    at more than £250,000 taken
        for Her Majesty *hanged* Ward
    in London for stealing a watch[11]

in America too the land
     snapped up by bankers
  driving farmers out

teaching the indignity
     of empty torn pockets
  amidst incomprehensible plenty

turning neighbors into paupers
     alms houses into jails
  part of the community

into odd and menacing
     figures we knew it would[12]
  unfold this way Rousseau

  told us so twenty-two years
     before Adam Smith's *Wealth of*
     Nations before Jefferson's

thundering *Declaration*
     in his *Discourse on Inequality*
  asking *how many crimes*

wars murders how much
     misery and horror
  the human race would have

been spared
     if only someone
  had shouted

no to the first landlord
     no to the first banker
  no to the first enforcer

who *enclosed a piece*
        of land and said
    This is mine

Rousseau feared the paradox
        capitalism rising conquering
    the Church the Aristocracy

freeing the bourgeoisie
        to ravish the globe
    shouting into the wind

    you are lost if you forget
            the fruits of the earth
        belong to everyone

    the earth belongs to
            no one but of course[13]
        it does from top to bottom

        The Octopus of wealth
                choking Norris's California
            farmers wailing in 1900

        they own us these
                taskmasters they own
            our homes they own

        our legislatures they own
                the ballot box
            they own the courts

        they are ruffians
                in politics ruffians
            in finance ruffians

in law ruffians
            in trade bribers
        swindlers tricksters

no outrage too great
            to daunt them no
        petty larceny too small

to shame them despoiling
            a government treasury
        of a million dollars

yet picking the pockets
            of a farmhand
        for the price

        of a loaf of bread[14]

IV. *La Isla de los Alcatraces*

Supertankers plow the Bay
            escorted by tug boats
        churning mounds of froth

leapt gracefully by sailboats
            angled down to the water
        skimming straining against

Bay wind ripping hats
            from the heads of tourists
        snapping photographs

the Brit behind me
            in line complaining
        for the love of God

the queue's bloody huge
    this glorious afternoon
  dreamlike Tiburon glimmering

across the choppy Bay
    Monterey Pines swaying
  in the breezy tidal magic

Sausalito full of vacationers
    swarming with cameras
  trolling for beers lattés

mussels lobster Blue Angels
    crushing the helpless sky
  with low sonic booms

rolling from Golden Gate
    to Mt. Tamalpais seeping
  unwelcome into consciousness

  my teeth chattering
    watching the sublime
  efficiency of destruction

  traced in vapor trails
    fading across the sky
  drunken Fleet Week

masses cheering power
    dives pulled up short
  before the glowing Bridge

at mach 6 a sidewinder
    can eliminate enemy defenses
  obliterate outposts batteries

before they see it
      before they hear it
    before they feel it

death is upon you
      as the fog burns
    off the Berkeley hills

the Campanile jutting
      out of the tangled mass
    across the Bay where

we appear as blurry dots
      beneath the Island's
    warning beacon flashing

    since 1854 amidst the apple[15]
        trees aloe century plants
      black raspberries clinging to

Alcatraz The Rock
      Alcatraz shit covering
    the island from pelicans

cormorants deer mice
      sea gulls black oyster catchers
    California slender salamanders

the last lingering life
      on *La Isla de los Alcatraces*
    The Island of the Pelicans

the Bay's most popular
      tourist site you need to buy
    tickets months in advance

$11 ferry ride includes
          headsets that shepherd
you around the Island

in synchronous fascination
          all nationalities ethnicities
classes ages all of us

enchanted by the theatre
          of punishment
     torture herds of tourists

shuffling to the next story
          whispering aghast to aunts
uncles children scurrying

     I can't believe it
               Yes I know How terrible
          Perhaps the Gift Shop

     will have a poster a hat a t-shirt
               something for the relatives
          who love *The Great Escape*

     The Birdman of Alcatraz
               Murder in the First Degree
          for only $5 your memory

preserved in wallet-size photos
          stand here between the bars
     for $3 you can rent these

costumes these hats
          these handcuffs
     smile ready OK?

you look perfect—there
  the folks will think
it's so funny

but I cannot laugh
  for fear of angering
  the spirits haunting this ground

If you listen closely
  you can hear the howls[16]
of those whose lives

were wasted here
  just now it was as if
  someone not alive

were watching[17]

V. *An Astonishing Array*

While we tourists roam
  the grounds of the past
where it seems the dead

are awake and so reach
  for each other stomachs[18]
churning heads spinning

eyes averted *denials were*
  their daily bread twisted[19]
concrete strewn at our feet

the CDC's PIA builds
  an empire of slave labor
24,000 varieties

of 1,800 different items
  An astonishing array
of goods with annual sales

of almost *$156 billion*[20]
  Professor George Goldman
from UC Berkeley

the world's largest
  weapons lab once my[21]
employer once my

colleague writes a report
  funded by the Prison Industrial
Authority claiming the impact

of prison labor on California is
  about the same as the State's
commercial fishing industry[22]

 like the Pelican Bay
  State Prison home of SHU
 The Security Housing Unit

 where *1,267 men* are doomed
  to perpetual solitary confinement[23]
 conditions so cruel Judge Henderson

 ruled in Madrid v. Gomez
  They lead to serious
 psychiatric consequences[24]

  but unlike the fishing industry
   the prison brings *$83.8 million*
  per year to sleepy Crescent City[25]

where *the contract*
   for hauling away
  the prison's garbage

is $130,000 a year
   the prison boom floating
  all boats in the rising tide

good pay good benefits
   county taxes doubling
  from $73 to $142 million

flush times for the lucky
   who drive by chained prisoners
  the new *public work crews*

labored *almost 150,000 hours*
   between 1990 and 1996
  saving the county $766,300

County Assessor Jerry Cochran admitting
   Without the prison
  we wouldn't exist[26]

  making it hard
    not to think
   of old Gene Debs

  proclaiming from Atlanta
    work behind prison walls
   is slavery[27]

  and the leased convicts
    on Jim Crow's chain gangs
   working the plantations

or my student Shaka speaking
calmly graced by
the wisdom of perspective

during slavery work was understood to be a punishment
and became despised as any punishment is despised
work became hated
as does any activity which accomplishes no reward
for the doer
work became identified with slavery
and slavery with punishing work
this is why I refuse

to work in the prison system
I unequivocally refuse
to be a slave[28]

E.J. countering
the real hardship
the life altering

apprehension is losing
the practice of working
toward a goal[29]

then Burkhart laughing
hands circling the air
rocking back in his chair

telling us stories about
the "saw jockeys" his graveyard
shift at the butcher's shop

man it was porkchop city
I'm covered in blood
turning the other way

when the poor kids
> *tucked some sausage*
> *in their baggy pants*

a happy blood-spattered
> Robin Hood for carnivores
> *I loved that job*

I paid my own way
> *didn't ask nobody*
> *for nothin'*

but this joint works
> *on lies and deals*
> *I'm afraid I've forgotten*

what it's like to earn
> *an honest day's pay for*
> *an honest day's work*[30]

> Paul Wright observing
>> *it's not really slave labor*
>> *it's more like serfdom*

or being a domesticated animal[31]
> and like zoos
> it's not clear

if it's slavery
> or serfdom or torture
> just cruel wasteful

the PIA working with slave
> wages *95 cents an hour*[32]
> no insurance no OSHA

no property taxes
        no union pressure
    still *losing $1.4 million*

in 1993 on sales of
        $128.6 million[33]
    like the profit-seeking

Correctional Corporation of
        America *the largest provider*
    of detention and correction

services with 65,000 beds
        in 70 facilities nationwide
    yet *lost from 1984 to 1986*

an aggregate of $6.8 million[34]
        yet times are flush
    for the architects of Hell

girdling the globe
        which explains why the CCA
    was purchased by Marriott

via Sodexho the French Conglomerate
        enabling CCA to go global
    building private prisons

in the USA France Britain
        Puerto Rico Australia
    net income $60 million in 1999 [35]

    leaving one stunned
        at the mass-production
    of pain misery horror

the manufacturing of evil
> while the dignity of work
is gutted and flayed

like Mr. Goldman's fish
> proving *these are the times*
of organized lunacy[36]

LOVE AND DEATH IN CALIFORNIA

For B.A.K., Richard Kamler, and my San Quentin Tutors

I. *Entrance*

Entering San Quentin prison is an elaborate introduction to a world of bureaucracy, steel, fear, and the mass-production of suffering. At the first gate, at the end of the long driveway on the East side of the prison, you show your identification to a guard who matches your particulars with a clearance form verifying that you have been approved to enter the prison—no clearance, no entrance. You are scanned here by a handheld wand that beeps at metal: belt buckles, shoe tips, watches, guns, knives, bombs. The guard's hut stands apart from the prison, a good quarter-mile from the main gate, and is full of thick black books containing clearance forms, regulations, protocols, the dead letters of a bureaucracy so vast that no one knows which rules are relevant and which ones have been superceded by last week's memo from the Director's Office in Sacramento regarding LC-27As. One rule that seems etched in stone, however, is that every vehicle leaving the prison must stop at the East Gate and open its trunk, whereupon the guard dutifully checks that spare tire, jack, jumper cables, and antifreeze have not been replaced by escaping prisoners, stolen office equipment, or the contraband that keeps the prison humming. The search generally consists of the guard helloing the driver, who pops the trunk, toward which the guard waves a quick look of annoyed concern—it takes but a moment and, if you didn't know what was happening, would look more like a strangely choreographed farewell ritual of a secret society than a serious security check. Nonetheless, vehicles driving out of the prison take precedence over volunteers walking into the prison (who park outside the East Gate), so one frequently finds

117

oneself standing outside the gates of the prison, waiting for the lone East
Gate guard to complete his searches before turning his attention to you.

The evening breezes lifting off the San Francisco Bay are cold and
wet, so once the sun slides behind Mount Tamalpais, commanding the
horizon to the West, and once the stream of guards heading home with
their dubious trunks peters out, the East Gate guards turn for comfort to
crackly radios and portable heaters, shivering in the cold of their lonely
outpost.

> *Hey, Johnson, how ya doin'?*
> *Evenin' fellas.*
> *Everything OK here?*
> *No complaints. No complaints.*
> *You guys gonna' lock down for the execution?*
> *You know it. Always do.*

The walk down the driveway is curious. To your far left is the sublime glory of the Bay, with Berkeley and Oakland shimmering across the
water; closer in, across the inlet where the commuter ferry docks, the
lights of Tiburon millionaires blink in and out of the fog. The view is
breathtaking. To your right is a line of houses rented to guards and ad-
ministrators. The first house on the walk has a hoop out front where kids
who wish they were taller, older, and badder bounce about in frantic circles play-shouting

> *Foul, foul, what a fuckin' hack job!*
> *Bring it on nigger, bring it strong!*
> *Aw man, what'd mom say 'bout that?*

There's an ATM. There are phone booths. And then there's the infamous
San Quentin watch tower, from which, if you make the mistake of running, hurried phone calls leap across the yard, sending guards toward
lockers full of high-powered rifles—*running is not advised*. At the end of
the driveway, beneath the tower, you again show identification, which is
again checked against clearance forms. If cleared, you walk through an
X-ray machine. Sometimes you are asked to walk through twice. Sometimes you are asked to take off your shoes. Sometimes your bag is

searched. Sometimes no one is there and you just walk through, thankful for a small reprieve.

After the X-ray machine you walk another fifty yards to the main gate, buried within the giant stone and steel fortress-like wall that marks the perimeter of the old prison grounds. In the front hallway you again show identification, which is again checked against clearance forms. If cleared for admittance you then sign your name into a log book. Signing the log book serves, among other things, as your acknowledgment that if you are taken hostage the state is not obligated to attempt your rescue. After signing-in your bag is again searched and your hand is stamped with an ultraviolet mark that only shows up when held under the right light—it's like getting ID-ed at a club. The walls here are pasted with fading photocopied memos about the Fishing Club's Sunday Luncheon, Officer of the Month announcements, job openings in administration, and various warnings about parking violations, new filing procedures, and monthly location reassignments. Like any other factory, the ends of shifts prompt swarms of workers to hurry for freedom, streaming through the gates in bunches. Some guards slump along, existentially suffering; others chatter excitedly as they push their way ahead, all energy, elbows, and attitude. Those of us who volunteer to teach, counsel, and tutor stand huddled to the side while uniforms of all shades and designs come and go:

> *Rackers, my man—*
> *Jumbo, dude!*
> *You shootin' Saturday?*
> *Saturday? Thought we was on fer Sunday?*

> *Hey Franco you check out Rodriguez in L-block?*
> *What the fuck was that?*
> *He's lookin' fer a 103 big time—*

> *Hell with that*
> *we should just*
> *bust some head*

When the crush dies down and the uniforms have all left, you enter the sally-port, a large room with massive steel-barred doors on front and back. A guard in an elevated observation booth off to one side pushes a button that makes a dull buzzing sound, the door clicks open, and you heave the gate aside, enter the room, and close the door behind you. On your right is a giant steel-plated door. Rumor has it that this is a dumb-waiter for weapons, one of the secure locations where guards know they can find firearms in sticky situations. After the first door slams shut, the guard again buzzes and the second door clicks open, you push your way out, heave closed the second door, and enter the grounds of the prison.

Late at night, after teaching, after talking about class, after making love, the sound of the steel doors clanging shut echoes through my mind in a haunting tape loop; over and over I hear Judith Tannenbaum's student, Spoon, describing his lying in bed after class:

> Restless, unable to sleep
> Keys, bars, guns being racked
> Year after year
> Endless echoes
> of steel kissing steel[1]

After teaching college in prisons for nine years, after passing through sally-ports on thousands of occasions, I have yet to come to terms with those sounds, yet I know the clanging steel doors and mechanical buzz-ing and guard chatter and haunting weapons cache of the sally-port will stand forever in my mind as symbols of the banality of evil, of the bu-reaucratic production of pain, of what hell we are capable of creating in the name of law and order.

II. *He Was a Good Man*

On Friday night, the 12th of February 1999, I entered San Quentin prison to teach my class. Jay Siripong had been executed four nights ear-lier at 12:01 AM Tuesday, one minute past midnight. Like many Califor-nians opposed to the death penalty, I spent that night outside the prison singing, chanting, shouting, praying, talking to my neighbors, holding my lover's hand, feeling my heart sink into the familiar nausea brought on by the violence of the law. Nonetheless, one of my students had writ-ten a particularly promising essay and we had arranged for my coming to the prison early to spend a half-hour working on his prose, trying to move the piece toward publishing. So despite the fact that I had spent Monday night outside the prison seething with rage, Friday night I walked into the prison as a teacher with a small yet necessary task: to teach a man who wanted to learn.

Because of my appointment with my student, I came to the prison earlier than usual, a little ahead of the hurried changing of shifts of guards. I usually entered the prison with my tutors—Brian, Cat, Todd, Jody, Adam, Shane, Hong, Nicole, over thirty of them over a three year period—kind, giving, joyous students from Berkeley who had volunteered to help teach the men in prison. We would walk in a loud, happy pack, joking about the entrance procedures, discussing class strategies, reveling in the sense of community built around our shared commitment to the liberatory promises of education and activism. But on this night I entered the prison alone. I found myself in the sally-port with three guards when one of the bells went off, signaling a stop in all movement—someone somewhere had just done something prompting a temporary "security situation." So there we were, both doors locked, hanging out in the sally-port.

There are three guards: an older, relaxed, veteran guard with a giant belly and snow-white hair; a middle-aged guard in green fatigues, edgy, cut like a football player; and a young kid, his uniform not fitting right, shifting his weight from foot to foot, clearly wondering to himself "what the fuck am I doing here?" The men radiate distinct energies: one is checked-out, one is angry, one is just confused. After some small talk, we begin to discuss Jay's execution. The young kid, who it turns out is in his second week of duty, thinks Jay got what he had coming:

Fuck 'em. He murdered those two in cold blood.

The veteran looks down on the boy:

I knew Jay. He was a good man.

The fatigue-clad guard shakes his head, smirking, grimacing in disbelief, telegraphing his vengeful solidarity with the young boy's position. The old guard continues:

> *There's some freaks up there on the row. Don't get me*
> *wrong. Men who did some evil shit. But Jay's not one of*
> *'em. He had some kinda' calm that man. Some kinda'*
> *peace. I'm tellin' ya, he was a good man.*

We talk in awkward circles for about twenty minutes. The young kid makes a joke about "the crazies" at the vigil. I tell him I was there. The fatigue-clad guard again grimaces:

> *Yeah, I was too. Wish I'd seen ya' so I could bust your*
> *faggot ass—*
>   *For shit's sake Joe, relax, it's nothing to get busted*
> *over, is it? Just a demonstration. Folks been doin' it for*
> *years and we ain't had any trouble.*

I wonder how many executions the old guard has witnessed? How many furious young men he's watched using their jobs in prison as a vehicle for releasing waves of inarticulate rage? How many clueless young kids he's seen come and go, repulsed by the subculture of violence and racism driving guard culture? How many professors he's walked to class across the yard, wondering what the hell we're doing there?

> *So, uh, how far in advance d' ya' have to put in for over-time—*
>   *Good god, son, why would you choose to be here when they*
> *do that?*
>   *So what you do instead?*
>   *I was making love with my wife, that's what. It's a simple*
> *choice, boys: love or death—which one you want more?*

III. *Thankful*

Balancing the joys of teaching in prison with the terrors of having to spend time in them has left me confused. I am sympathetic with those prison activists who refuse to set foot in prisons, yet cannot begin to convey how joyous it is to watch men who have never before been validated in ideas, writing, and speech come to life, come to power, come to self-realization through learning. Despite whatever political conclusions one may wish to draw about the criminal-industrial-complex in general and the death penalty in particular, I must confess that the more horror I have come to see in those two forces, the more I have come to cherish the simple kindness that flows between two people when talking about a book or an essay or a sentence. There is something redeeming in that small moment, when class, race, age, and circumstance give way to common understanding, when confusion and fear give way to a humble, awestruck thankfulness.

Execution vigils in particular have come to seem to me more than political demonstrations where we bear witness to state-sanctioned murder. I have come to see them as public occasions for practicing compassion, as moments where citizens come together to envision what our world might be like if not driven by the mass-production of fear, pain, and suffering. And while there are any number of political possibilities involved in that coming together of citizens, in the wonderful talking that takes place between Vietnam vets and nuns and students and mothers and neighbors at the vigils, I have come to recognize that my most intense energies at these events are directed toward my wife, Brett. I find myself at execution vigils clinging to her almost desperately. It is as if in the face of both an impending murder and the overwhelming political odds stacked against our fight against the death penalty, our loving each other serves as the foundation, as the beginning place from where any new politics of caring engagement might begin. The more my political and pedagogical commitments place me in proximity with horror, the more I feel the need to love her—it is not a retreat or an escape, but a delicate form of balancing the personal and the political, a simple and beautiful reminder that we are capable of so much more.

This is all new to me. I have been working as a prison activist for a dozen years now, so I am well-practiced in the arts of street theatre, marching and demonstrating, in the channeling of political anger, yet I have only been *learning how to love* relatively recently. I find it all somewhat fuzzy. But I cannot deny how powerfully I feel this sense that loving Brett is somehow the only way to make it through such moments without losing my bearings, without getting lost in bitterness. It seems to me, then, that death as a natural physical fact is not so much an issue as is *living in the shadow of state-sanctioned murder*, which cannot help but force us to think more deeply about living, about how we love and how we move through days haunted by violence.

IV. *Love is the Enchantment*

From the Campanile stunned
   fog-bound Bay sky falling
  distracted rain across our faces

hair wet tangled wrapped
   'round raw ears noses fingers
  time insufficient to honor

such inexpressible joy
   your effortless grace
  beyond language

my babbling from fear
   the shock of knowing
  for the first time

the beautiful vulnerability
   of needing loving
  without doubt finally

embodying after 35 years
   the uncompromised clarity
  of Emerson's vision

  love is the enchantment
    of human life
   it is sacred

  it makes all things alive
    and significant opening[2]
   forgiveness into kindness

  the veil of resignation *sadness*
    Schelling's regret evaporated[3]
   with Walt I stand amazed

I cannot be awake
        for nothing looks to me
    as it did before

or else I am awake
        for the first time[4]
    we tremble together

your strong arms blessing
        me your gentle beauty
    transcending consciousness

in the pleasure of belief
        the most basic worship
    the knowing of the body[5]

your hands on my shoulders
        my hands on your face
    moving transfixed

enveloped in *the soft*
        bending arch of recognition[6]
    friendship's *grammar of grace*[7]

sliding toward *sacred thrill*
        Kant's sublime *amazement*
    bordering on terror expanding

the imagination towering[8]
        above red clay tiled roofs
    trading stories of Rome

Avignon Madrid layering
        promises amidst thundering
    chimes noontime concertos

we rock gently within the wind
            on *the intricate balconies of breath*
        overlooking the rest of our lives[9]

V. *An Application of Capital*

There are times when meaning
        is so profound one is
    indifferent to happiness or death[10]

like yesterday's waves
            of gentle epiphanies
        amidst afternoon rain

helloing our neighbors
            along Lake Merritt
        amidst eucalyptus and mud

Oakland hills melting
            into clouds absorbing sky
        swirling textured grays

sweet rain beading on your umbrella
            talk of Rousseau Voltaire
        circling towards 1515 Webster

a street named for greatness
                Mr. Webster eloquent Whig
        prudent opponent of slavery

challenging Southern adventurism
                the colossal outrage of theft
        war with Mexico orchestrated

by cotton elites seeking land
                Mr. W. countering in Congress
        The country is already large enough[11]

Secretary of State Congressman
     Senator lawyer's lawyer
  tongue so sharp

the children read folktales
     of the all-night debate
  where he whipped the devil[12]

conservative hierarchical democrat
     blessing capitalism's onslaught
  as *An application of capital*

to the benefit of all[13]
     while accepting kickbacks
  from Biddle's Second U.S. Bank[14]

for defending modernity progress
     high finance against provincial
  King Andrew Indian Killer

elegant YWCA opened in 1915
     the city flowing with war-
money dock-yards booming

democracy's promise redeemed
     through Julia Morgan
  graduate of UC Berkeley

Engineering class of '04
     the first California woman
  licensed as an architect

her graceful arches stairways
     Greco-Roman columns
  circling the second floor

balcony where single mothers
 AIDS counseling aerobics
grassroots politics flourish

feeding the spirit of young women
 offering kindness compassion[15]
for neighbors strangers ourselves

where we meet Sonja Richard Judy
 Sean Naneen Josh Shelly Robin
the Bay Area movement folk

gathered together clinging
 to hope each other the dream
of justice drawing us

to celebrate Jay Siripong's resolve[16]
 not the images derivative simple
lifted from *National Geographic*

but his meditative process
 creating beauty peace calm
amidst terror the ferocity

of a State that kills
 over 200 gassed 308 hung
from José Gabriel the first

a 60-year-old indigent laborer
 Mexican-Indian his neck snapped
3 March 1893 by *a rope*

stretched for over a year
 by a 200 pound weight
to eliminate sagging[17]

to the most recent Jay
   executed 12:01 AM
 9 February 1999 with

sodium pentothal
 to put him to sleep

  pancuronium bromide
   to stop his breathing

   potassium chloride
    to stop his heart[18]

on a bitterly cold Monday night
   Bay rain driving horizontally
 TV camera crews huddled

beneath tarps atop surrounding
   buildings flood lights on off on
 for each shoot the anchor

bored angry mumbling
   fussing over her makeup
 suddenly cheerful bubbly

when the lights flash on
   for another thirty second
 blast of disinformation

smearing another convict
   to be slaughtered
  by the taxes of the kindly[19]

streaming down on demonstrators
   chanting holding candles
 aloft in the freezing rain

each one snuffed out
   wax dripping onto gloves
  dyed by inks running

from posters warped and ripped
   monks nuns clerics Panthers
  teachers children students mothers

we stand in disbelief nauseous
   confused shifting soaking feet
  Marx running through my head

 Is there not a necessity
   for deeply reflecting
  upon an alteration

 of the system
   that breeds crimes
  while *glorifying the hangman*

 who executes criminals
   only to make room
  for the supply of new ones?[20]

then Mr. Hobbes's warning
   Glorying in the hurt of another
  is vainglory and contrary to reason

it *tendeth to the introduction*
   of warre amongst men
  and *is commonly stiled cruelty*[21]

 hell yes better the fiery spectacle
   of torture madness *warre cruelty*
  than the bureaucratic machinery

of a quiet doctor-assisted sleep
        reported by pancaked puppets
    in studied tones of sincerity

better the lions than lethal injection
        the *meticulous choreography of murder*[22]
    turned into painless obligation

    it's butchery after all
            let's see the *head bobbing*
        throat gurgling with blood

    eyebrows singed ashes falling
            flames shooting six inches
        from a smoked brain

    like Florida's Jessie Tafero
            electrocuted 4 May 1990
        now that's an execution[23]

VI. *Kant's Imagined Cosmos*

After Jay's exhibit we stroll
        along Lake Shore admiring
    the trees draped in party lights   -

the simple genius of community
        in the evening café a young man
    runs in frantic disheveled

customers look away
        snap judgments about skin coat
    hair blocking thought compassion

he sees my notepad and exclaims
        I just got some lyrics
    and gotta write 'em down

man I'll pay a dollar
        for a sheet of paper
    —My friend music transcends money

here take ten sheets
        and write well
    —Thank you God Bless you

—Oh let's leave Him
        out of it shall we?
    I wish I'd not said that

    you look up from your Diderot
            smiling Franklinesque above glasses
        gently your hand on my knee

    between us the unspeakable sickness
            Jay's imminent murder hanging
        in the air nestled between us

        still it brings me such joy
                just to look at you
            making love an extension

        of the nudge at the crosswalk
                the secret hand in the library
            each moment a promise

    of devotion
            each touch a gift
        of generosity

            illuminating the *systematic structure*
                    of Kant's imagined *cosmos*
                driven by nature's secret plan

compromised by
>   *heartless competitive vanity*
>   *the insatiable desire to possess*

oscillating between *a hell of evils*[24]
>   another glorious Oakland afternoon
>   our new friend's joyous creation

>   running down the street singing
>   >   lyrics celebrating freedom
>   and Jay's impending murder

>   >   inescapable paradoxes
>   >   >   propelling consciousness
>   >   toward aporia redeemed

>   for a moment by your
>   >   beauty teaching me
>   like Walt *I am larger*

>   >   *better than I thought*
>   >   >   *I did not know I held*
>   >   *so much goodness*

>   >   *All seems beautiful*
>   >   >   *to me* slowly opening[25]
>   >   onto the simple

>   grace of loving
>   >   building hope in the face
>   of another murder

>   >   in the name of law

VISITING MARIO

For Mario Rocha, Robin Sohnen, and Sister Janet Harris

I. *"Somewhere Near Salinas, Lord"*[1]

ten-thousand sprinklers spin
      in overlapping circles
   soaking row upon row

reflecting January morning sun
      as ocean fog evaporates
   filling the tangy air

with glistening fractured light
      spilling blinding beauty
   across the squinting valley

   the sun rose today
      in so many colors
   it nearly broke my heart[2]

   holding so much joy
      against so much pain
   we're visiting Mario

Chagall's stained-glass dreamscapes
      now but a naturalist's diary
   of the blessed colors painting

hills drenching trees glazing
          tractors mile-long mounds of
artichokes garlic strawberries

     where Cezar Chavez Saul Alinsky
               Dolores Huerta Fred Ross Gilbert Padilla
          Luis Valdez lefties Oakies spics

     union organizers suspected by the FBI
               of *Communist Infiltration*
          of the National Farm Workers Association

     rallied behind *El Malcriado*
               the fieldworkers' paper
          named after *the ill-bred one*s

     who feed the world
               marching with Bobby Kennedy
          in the hopeful days of '66³

roasting slowly beneath Pinnacles' peaks
          caves ravines where snorting pigs ramble
     kings of the Diablo Mountains

the Central Valley's cosmic bounty
          ticks rhythmically past car windows
     in grids diagonals hypnotizing

patterns broken by irrigation ditches
          fire roads fruit stalls swarming
     bargain-hunting Bay Area chefs

hauling bushels of brussel sprouts
          tubs of creamed honey bags of dates
     jars of sweet pickled jalapeños

back to air-conditioned SUVs
          shiny new Mercedes daddy's
     hand-me-down Beemer

en route to quarterly reports
        meditative hot-bath retreats
at Eselen Monterey Big Sur

gliding along 101
        past crews of *illegales*
hunched in the shade
        of battered pickups

California is a garden of Eden
a paradise to live in or see
but believe it or not
you won't find it so hot
if you ain't got that do-re-mi

if you ain't got that do-re-mi boy
if you ain't got that do-re-mi
you better get back to beautiful Texas
Oklahoma Kansas Georgia Tennessee[4]

drinking water from plastic jugs
        hats propped on knees leathery
hands scarred from lifetimes

of harvesting the glory
        of California
        for five dollars a day

II. *Falsely Accused, Wrongly Arrested, Unjustly Jailed*

Born in the East LA barrio of Highland Park
        to a junkie father a drunkard brother
and a saintly mother admired by all

who know her struggle to save her son
        from the stupid cycle of gangs cops
jail killing creativity smearing honor

Mario was placed in accelerated classes
        on the fast track to genius and success
    but was threatened by gang-bangers

so he faked difficulties with books
        he read in two languages over lunch
    pretended not to care about learning

and ran with bejeweled hipsters
        dealing crack stealing cars fucking
    stoned little girls skipping class

but Mario couldn't do it
        didn't have the stomach
    found the machismo too crude

so they gave him a spraycan
        let his imagination run wild
    tagging his way to safety

not getting into trouble with the law
        local gangs who knew he was
    too kind to hurt anyone

too smart to step into the death dance
        of the *California Youth Authority*
    a $380 million a year plantation

    47% Mexican 30% Black
        teaching *10,000 juveniles* each
    year how to be better criminals[5]

so he kept his distance
        kept up appearances
    tagging after studying

running with thugs
        he thought were his friends
    while dreaming of escape

party at *5806 Ebey Avenue*[6]
        grooves and kegs and chicks
    the -----s crash the fun

looking for the fuck-up
        who sold on their turf
    wearing the wrong cap

    just a business problem
        just a question of distribution
    a snag in *grassroots enterprise*

    an established part of the social structure
        of a 'hood where in the late 60s
    only 54% earned salaries and wages[7]

but too much drink
        leads to posturing
    a punch is thrown

somebody slammed into me
        a gun appears
    and ----- is shot dead

    Mario's in the backyard chillin'
        working on ----- from Chemistry
    she's impressed that he gets it

    thought he was just another joker
        but he knows the table of elements
    she's diggin' that thinks he's cute

    they're riffing on
        Orwell DuBois Civil Rights
    she's looking at him differently

he's getting ideas *this is good*
this could be righteous she's
hot and smart and who knows

when shots ring out
they dive to the ground
his hand on her bare shoulder

confused scared excited
so much pain
so much pleasure

her arms are strong she is so fine
Mario wants to forget the shots
and kiss her there clinging to the grass

kids scatter in every direction
bottles breaking on the driveway
tires screaming as cars peel away

everyone runs
the only thing worse
than getting plugged

getting picked up
by LA cops
looking for trouble

another fucked up night
in the barrio
party ruined
girl lost
homeboy dead
sirens serenade Mario to sleep

the trial a sham a charade
coerced testimony manufactured evidence
incompetent defense racist judge

three witnesses
      ID Mario Rocha
as the shooter

Mr. V the life-long stoner
who smoked marijuana every day
for seven years preceding his testimony
has since recanted
      I cannot and could
           not identify Mario
      as the shooter

Mr. M who was *relieving himself*
when the shooting occurred
and did not see who fired a gun
    and who later changed his story
    under suspected *unlawful coercion*
        has since testified that he
        was completely plastered
        and was so busy fighting
        that he *only got a glimpse*
        of the shooter

Mr. P said he heard 11 or 12 shots fired
but *only two bullets were recovered*
he swore he saw Mario do it
    but his friend Ms. N says he's wrong
        says they were on the backporch
        grooving to *Valerie's Dancing*
            when shots were fired in the driveway
        so Mr. P *could not*
            have identified the shooter

three scared young men
      not given the benefit of counsel
    their words twisted

their memories fogged
        no physical evidence found
    no known motive

Ms. A testified that Mario wasn't involved
    Ms. B testified that Mario wasn't involved
        Mr. C testified that Mario wasn't involved
            Ms. D testified that Mario wasn't involved
                Mr. E testified that Mario wasn't involved

48 letters testify that Mario wasn't involved

everyone knows he didn't do it
        even Detective Peterson
    telling Mario's Aunt

I know he's innocent
You tell me
who did the murder
Tell us and
I'll let Mario go home

but Mario doesn't know
        his Auntie doesn't know
    only bangers know

and they're not talking
        everyone needs a scapegoat
    Mario the fall guy

double life plus 26
means Mario
will die in prison

III. *The Bulldog Will Not Kill Today*

Salinas Valley State Prison
  300 acres of maximum security
 pain *$93 million* per year for

4,093 men a warehouse
  built in 1996 for 2,024
 held by *732 custody staff*

388 support service staff[8]
  shaded by giant eucalyptus
 moaning in the breeze

 two rows per pod
 twelve cells per row
 each cell with two bunks
 one stainless-steel toilet
 one stainless-steel sink
 one stainless-steel mirror
 all mounted to concrete walls

 immovable unbreakable
 impervious to fire
 one 2" slatted window
 glazed dark

  blocking the rhythm of the sky
   cheating the solace of the stars
  closing *the one portal to the world*

 is *the cruelest blow*
  robbing *another piece*
 of one's humanity[9]

A B C & D pods surrounded
  by a fifteen-foot-high electric fence
 transformers crackling with death

reinforced on both sides
        by razor-wire-topped chain-link walls
    separated from crackling juice

by ten feet of white crushed gravel
        motion sensors to detect the invisible
    dogs trained to eat human flesh

the terrible symmetry
        of maximum security
    creating order from chaos

        razor-wire
          stones
           juice
          stones
        razor-wire

clearly impossible to escape
yet the perimeter ringed
by guard towers manned by ex-Marines
armed with automatic rifles
dreaming of *AuthenTec*'s newest toy

fingerprint recognition systems
        biometric authentication techniques
    projected sales of $594 million by 2003[10]

and the Pentagon's newest *$40 million* toy
        built *to influence motivational behavior*
    an *active denial system* mounted on a Humvee

firing bursts of electromagnetic energy
        creating an intense burning sensation
    a *Crowd-Dispersal Weapon*[11]

perfect for prison walkways
        policed by guards in military uniforms
    with padded elbows shoulders

chauffeured in golf carts
      laughing their way back to processing
where the afternoon shift shuffles out

as we loved ones linger in line
      triplicate visiting forms
and driver's licenses in hand

clutching see-through zip-lock bags
      full of quarters waiting to buy
our sons and husbands and friends

a special lunch
      from one of three
vending machines

some microwave three-beef burrito
      some ham and provolone Italian sub
some sauce-included tub of hot wings

the visiting room reeking
      with the plastic stench
of melted grease

a hundred bags
      of microwaved popcorn
petrified processed cheese food

    hardened to the table
      from which Juan is pulled
    for kissing his wife

    next to the table
      where Reverend Hanson is warned
    about holding hands
      even when praying

next to the table
                    where Mario and Robin and I sit
          dazed by absurdity

by a $93 million per year facility
          with no toilet paper
no paper towels

I watch the slump shouldered
          65-year-old grandmother
who drove four hours from East LA

to see her boy
          thankful for small things
happy he's alive

her gang-banging grandson
          catching the rage in her eye
the edge in her voice
                    asking *Abuelita Abuelita*
          que paso? que hay?

everyone's struggling to be
          cheerful in the face of terror
pretending not to know

about the *sexual victimizations*
          striking *1 in 5 men*
1 in 4 women
                    especially the young
          who suffer *forced sex*
                    incidents while incarcerated[12]

or the *return rate with new prison term* of *13.2%*
or the *return rate as parole violator* of *54.5%*[13]

meaning seven of ten who enters these walls
          will never again lead normal lives
will never again be free

instead slipping into
      the river of the damned
   162,533 prisoners in 2000
         making California the largest prison
      colony in the world

everyone wondering if the indignity
      is planned or just bad management
    finding it impossible not to be cynical

as everyone is weeping
      now for no reason
    now for all reasons

the experience too much
      for anything other than tears
    or silence shaking your body

The Nausea consuming thought
      spilling into your mouth
    biting acidic burning

the old Mexican woman sobs
      as her boy is cuffed
  and taken back to hell

the Vietnamese couple whispers
      to their son nervous edgy
  looking over their hunched shoulders

checking to see
      if any Bulldogs have entered
  enforcers bullies extortionists

one can never be too sure
      they're killing machines
    cold-blooded murderers

the feared one sees his daughter
     crawling atop splattered ketchup packets
he scoops her up in a sweeping motion

cradling her in giant hands
     tattoos flexing
as his biceps ripple

     another of the *721,500 parents*
          of minor children in prison
     leaving *1,498,800* kids without

     either their mom or dad
          70% of those prisoners
     with no high school diploma[14]

     proving another of Gene Debs's points
          it is the family the judge sentences
     when he sends the man to prison[15]

I'm not sure
     if he's going to eat her
or splatter her brains out

by killing the dazed Norteño
     who's strayed into his path
smashing his daughter
     into the boy's forehead

there's a hush as he hesitates
     the rookie guard inches closer
the veterans smile
     awaiting the slaughter

     but the child laughs
          the Bulldog laughs
     his grandmama laughs

> everyone sighs
> > thankful the Bulldog
> > will not kill today

IV. *"There Must be Some Purpose"*

Sister Janet sees the fire
> knows he's got it
> grabs him by the arm

young man you're taking this class
> *don't even try it*
> *don't think you can pretend anymore*[16]

within two weeks he's written his first play
> by the end of the month he's writing poems
> the quiet kid from Highland Park becoming

a Juvenile Hall visionary
> the peoples' poet stunned
> to learn of a nation of prisoners

parolees house arrests broken lives
> *5.7 million adults under some form*
> *of correctional supervision in 1997*[17]

surrounded by hopelessness
> Mario miraculously begins writing
> from anger with love for hope

smiling comfortably possessed
> by unworldly calm
> between pretzels he says

I must have been put here
> *for some higher purpose*
> *to learn something true*

like Charlie Liteky
        shipped to Lompoc Federal Pen
    my favorite repeat offender

doing time this time
        for protesting Fort Benning's
    School of the Americas

    the infamous School of Assassins
            known throughout Latin America
        as la escuela de golpes

    the school of coups
        recently renamed by
      the poets of the Pentagon
            as *The Western Hemisphere*
            Institute for Strategic Cooperation[18]

Charlie watches bluejays
        swoop down for crumbs
turning refuse into life[19]

    like Chuck Culhane
        recalling how in Sing Sing Prison
    the birds woke me up

with their clamorous love
        wings beating around the bars
   in the rush of lusty spring[20]

Charlie again serving time
        as spiritual mentor to prisoners
practicing Debs's dignity

of paying the price
        in *Cell No. 4 Range No. 7 Cellhouse B* [21]
    for uncompromised commitment

not necessarily the way I want
or aspire to walk but
the path I am led to[22]

on New Year's Eve
        his cellies are *disappeared*
    vanished evaporated

reminding Charlie *how it must feel*
        for third country families
    whose loved ones are disappeared

        by paramilitary death squads[23]
                led by Argentine navy commander
            Adolfo Francisco Scilingo

    dumping tortured civilians
            many still alive
        out of helicopters

    into the freezing *Atlantic*
            1,500 to 2,000 murdered
        between 1977 and 1978 [24]

    or Guatemalan intelligence officer
            Colonel Julio Roberto Alpirez
        a graduate of *la escuela de golpes*

    who tortured and executed
            Efrain Bamaca Velasquez
        during the purges of '92[25]

yet in the face of nightly
        horror kindness persists
    in the form of *sharing*

an orange apple radio basketball shoes
         the best is the sharing of oneself
we all guard against abuse[26]

when the Elder leaves the prison
         Charlie is asked to lead
Sweat Lodge Services

for Sioux activists
         enabling him to learn
the beauty of First People's ethics

each morning when you arise
         each evening before sleep
give thanks for life

the hurt of one is the hurt
         of all the honor of one is
the honor of all[27]

like Mario turning
         pain into wisdom
like Sister Helen
         singing softly
         her hands pressed against the glass
              of the execution chamber

         I will be with you
         I will be with you
         All around Him
         Gather us around[28]

Mario our love receive
         our wishes welcome
our thanks embrace

for embodying hope
         it is a privilege my friend
to encounter dignity[29]

as we whisper along
      with Dar's tribute
   to Father Daniel Berrigan

I had no right
      but for the love of you
   oh it's a long road

     from law to justice[30]

KARINA'S QUESTION

For Karina Epperlein, Buzz Alexander, and our colleagues in
The Blue Mountain Artists Against Massive Incarceration

Morningbirds call from steamy treetops
        towering above a rain-swollen creek
splashing through heavy high grass

as fog lifts above the hills
        beyond the lake
stitched together by jagged lines

of reflected blue-green
        late-Spring birches melt
into tender white blossoms

entwining with sheaths
        of Adirondack slate gray bark
and swarms of black flies

abolitionists squeak downstairs
        with fuzzy morning faces
looking for coffee and the first hello

as a wall of rain advances across the lake
        smelled first then heard before seen
bouncing off the water on its way

to engulfing the house
        in a welcome blast
of fresh wet cold

the new abolitionists are confused
        searching artists dancers musicians poets
teachers organizers from San Francisco

Miami New York Ann Arbor Duluth
        Austin every neighborhood of every town
across America where children are lonely

and wives are beaten and lost men
        simmer in another drunken stew
of frustration and violence born of

500 years of mass-produced fear
        Karina recalling her grandparents'
flight from the Holocaust

asks for the cream please
        and begins breakfast
with the observation

We're imperfect people
        and we don't know
what to do

but something must
        be done what will
our grandchildren say?

NOTES

Introduction

1. From the preface to the original, 1855 version of Whitman's *Leaves of Grass* (New York: n.p., 1855), vi; for critical commentary see Stephen Hartnett, *Democratic Dissent & The Cultural Fictions of Antebellum America* (Champaign: University of Illinois Press, 2002), 132-172; for a similar call for a return to a Whitmanesque ethos in political poetry see June Jordan, "For the Sake of a People's Poetry: Walt Whitman and The Rest of Us," in *Poetry and Politics: An Anthology of Essays*, ed. Richard Jones (New York: Quill, 1985), 188-199.

2. Ralph Waldo Emerson, "The Poet" (1884), in *Ralph Waldo Emerson: Selected Essays*, ed. Larzer Ziff (New York: Penguin, 1982), 202; for an example of how far contemporary poetry has strayed from Emerson's vision, lumbering ever closer to tenured cynicism and polished obscurantism, see the second half of Jerome Rothenberg and Pierre Joris, eds., *Poems of the Millenium, The University of California Book of Modern and Postmodern Poetry, Volume Two: From Postwar to Millennium* (Berkeley: University of California Press, 1998).

3. Sven Birkerts, "'Poetry' and 'Politics,'" *Margin* 4 (Autumn 1987): 55, where Birkerts demonstrates his allegiance to a traditional version of the former and an emaciated version of the latter; for more empowering responses to this question, see the essays collected in Jones, *Poetry and Politics;* for more experimental responses see the works in Charles Bernstein, ed., *The Politics of Poetic Form: Poetry and Public Policy* (New York: Roof, 1990), and in Jonathan Monroe, ed., "Poetry, Community, Movement," a special issue of *diacritics* 26:3 & 4 (fall-winter 1996).

4. From Mario Rocha's "Four Years Down Today," *Broken Chains* (Summer 2001): 11; these lines were written on the anniversary of Mario's wrongful incarceration, while doing time in the Salinas Valley State Prison. For details on his case see "Visiting Mario," included

herein; to contact him, write to Mario Rocha, #K91379, Calipatria State Prison, P.O. Box 5002, Calipatria, CA 92233.

5. See Dwight Conquergood, "Homeboys and Hoods: Gang Communication and Cultural Spaces," in *Group Communication in Context: Studies of Natural Groups*, ed. Larry Frey (Hillsdale, N.J.: Erlbaum, 1994), 23-55, and "Between Rigor and Relevance: Rethinking Applied Communication," in *Applied Communication in the 21st Century*, ed. Kenneth Cissna (Mahwah, N.J.: Erlbaum, 1995), 79-96; Larry Frey, Barnett Pearce, Mark Pollock, Lee Artz, and Bren Murphy, "Looking for Justice in All the Wrong Places: On a Communication Approach to Social Justice," *Communication Studies* 47 (1996): 117, 111; for an example of Frey's work pursuing these imperatives see Mara Adelman and Frey, *The Fragile Community: Living Together with AIDS* (Mahwah, N.J.: Earlbaum, 1997); for my own contribution to this dialogue, see "Lincoln and Douglas Engage the Abolitionist David Walker in Prison Debate: Empowering Education, Applied Communication, and Social Justice," *The Journal of Applied Communication Research* 26 (1998): 232-253.

6. Pierre Bourdieu, "For a Scholarship with Commitment," in *Profession 2000*, ed. Phyllis Franklin (New York: Modern Language Association, 2000), 42; Elaine Scary, "Beauty and the Scholar's Duty to Justice," *Ibid.*, 21; for aligned arguments see the essays collected in Carol Becker, ed., *The Subversive Imagination: Artists, Society, & Social Responsibility* (New York: Routledge, 1994) and in the special issue of *Rhetoric & Public Affairs* 5:2 (Summer 2002) dedicated to deliberative democracy.

7. Dwight Conquergood, "Beyond the Text: Toward a Performative Cultural Politics," in *The Future of Performance Studies: Visions and Revisions*, ed. Sheron Dailey (Annandale, Va.: National Communication Association, 1998), 26, 27; and see Conquergood, "Ethnography, Rhetoric, and Performance," *Quarterly Journal of Speech* 78 (1992): 80-97; for examples of this turn toward ethnography and performance (with mixed results), see the work over the past fifteen years in *Text and Performance Quarterly*, one of the National Communication Association's journals; one of the many touchstones for this turn toward ethnography and performance is Michel de Certeau, *The Practice of Everyday Life*, trans. Steven Rendell (1975; Berkeley: University of California Press, 1984);

and see the encyclopedic collection of essays in Norman Denzin and Yvonna Lincoln, eds., *Handbook of Qualitative Research, Second Edition* (Thousand Oaks, Calif.: Sage, 2000).

8. From Ed Lipman, "Matrix III," in *The Light From Another Country: Poetry from American Prisons*, ed. Joseph Bruchac (Greenfield, N.Y.: Greenfield Review Press, 1984), 194; Lipman wrote these lines in 1971, while in Folsom Prison.

9. From David Bowman, "Untitled 1," *Correction(s)* 1:1 (Fall 2001), 5; Bowman wrote these lines in 2000 while incarcerated in the Brown Creek Correctional Facility in Polk County, North Carolina.

10. From "Tetrina," by the Bedford Hills Writing Workshop, 1996, in *Doing Time: 25 Years of Prison Writing—A PEN American Center Prize Anthology*, ed. Bell Gale Chevigny (New York: Arcade, 1999), 113.

11. H. Bruce Franklin, ed., *Prison Writing in 20th-Century America* (New York: Penguin, 1998), 1; for an internationalist collection of prisoner writings see Siobhan Dowd, ed., *This Prison Where I Live: The PEN Anthology of Imprisoned Writers* (London: Cassell, 1996).

12. Raylene Hinz-Penner, *Out of The Blue Book* (Hutchinson, Kans.: n.p., 2001), first unnumbered leaf; on Franklin's work see notes 11 and 14; on Chevigny see note 9; Marilla Arguelles, ed., *Extracts from Pelican Bay* (Berkeley: Pantograph, 1995); Wilbert Rideau and Ron Wikberg, eds., *Life Sentences: Rage and Survival Behind Bars* (New York: Times Books, 1992), and see *The Farm*, Rideau's award-winning 1998 documentary about Angola Prison; to find Adams and *Correction(s)* go to www.prisonerswrite.org; contact Dick Shelton and *Walking Rain Review* at P.O. Box 85462, Tucson AZ 85754-5462; contact Tory Samartino and *Voices Unbroken* at voicesunbroken@yahoo.com; contact Raylene Hinz-Penner and *Out of The Blue Book* at Rhpenner@bethelks.edu.

13. Carolyn Forché, "Ourselves or Nothing," in *The Country Between Us* (New York: Perennial, 1981), 59.

14. See H. Bruce Franklin, *Prison Literature in America: The Victim as Criminal and Artist* (New York: Oxford University Press, 1989); see the catalogue of Bruchac's works available at www.josephbruchac.com; Sister Helen Prejean, from the Foreword to *Doing Time*, xi; Judith Tannenbaum, *Disguised as a Poem: My Years Teaching Poetry at San Quentin* (Boston: Northeastern University Press, 2000), 91—and see the

catalogue of chapbooks produced by Tannenbaum's prison students at www.chapbooks.prisonwall.org.

15. See David Rothman, *The Discovery of the Asylum: Social Order and Disorder in the New Republic* (Boston: Little, Brown, 1971); Michel Foucault, *Discipline & Punish: The Birth of the Prison* (1975; New York: Vintage, 1995); Karen Halttunen, *Murder Most Foul: The Killer and the American Gothic Imagination* (Cambridge: Harvard University Press, 1998); Marie Christine Leps, *Apprehending the Criminal: The Production of Deviance in Nineteenth Century Discourse* (Durham, N.C.: Duke University Press, 1992); John Sloop, *The Cultural Prison: Discourse, Prisoners, and Punishment* (Tuscaloosa, Ala.: University of Alabama Press, 1996); Nils Christie, *Crime Control as Industry: Towards Gulags, Western Style, Second Edition* (London: Routledge, 1994); Jeffrey Reiman, *The Rich Get Richer and the Poor Get Prison: Ideology, Class, and Criminal Justice, Third Edition* (New York: Macmillan, 1990); David Shichor, *Punishment for Profit: Private Prisons/Public Concerns* (Thousand Oaks, Calif.: Sage, 1995); Daniel Burton-Rose, ed., *The Celling of America: An Inside Look at the U.S. Prison Industry* (Monroe, Maine: Common Courage, 1998); Steven Donziger, ed., *The Real War on Crime: The Report of the National Criminal Justice Commission* (New York: Harper Perennial, 1996); Christian Parenti, *Lockdown America: Police and Prisons in the Age of Crisis* (London: Verso, 1999).

16. There are many schools of thought regarding these questions; for introductions from a variety of perspectives see Stephen Bronner and Douglas Kellner, eds., *Passion and Rebellion: The Expressionist Heritage* (South Hadley, Mass.: Bergin, 1983); Dailey, *The Future of Performance Studies;* Hal Foster, ed., *The Anti-Aesthetic: Essays on Postmodern Culture* (Port Townsend, Wash.: Bay Press, 1983); Frederic Jameson, ed., *Aesthetics & Politics: Debates Between Bloch, Lukacs, Brecht, Benjamin, Adorno* (London: Verso, 1977); and Herbert Marcuse, *The Aesthetic Dimension: Toward a Critique of Marxist Aesthetics* (Boston: Beacon Press, 1978).

17. All further Dos Passos references are cited in the text and refer to *Nineteen Nineteen* (1932; New York: Signet, 1969); for a glowing reading see Jean-Paul Sartre, "John Dos Passos and *1919*" (1938), in *Literary Essays* (New York: Wisdom Library, 1957), 88-96.

18. Dos Passos's moving tribute to Bourne is in *1919*, 119-121; the phrase "war is the health of the state" is probably familiar to many readers as the title to chapter fourteen of Howard Zinn's *A People's History of the Unites States* (New York: Perennial, 1980), 350-367; for more in-

formation on Bourne see Leslie Vaughan, *Randolph Bourne and the Politics of Cultural Radicalism* (Lawrence: University of Kansas Press, 1997).

19. The literature on historical methods is vast and could fill an entire book on its own; for recent contributions see, on rhetorical history, Hartnett, *Democratic Dissent*, 1-39; on music, Robert Branham and Stephen Hartnett, *Sweet Freedom's Song: "My Country 'Tis of Thee" and Democracy in America* (Oxford: Oxford University Press, 2002); on poetry, Edward Sanders, *America: A History in Verse, Volume I: 1900-1939* (Santa Rosa, Calif.: Black Sparrow, 2000); and on photography, Cara Finnegan, *Picturing Poverty: Print Culture and FSA Photographs* (Washington, D.C.: Smithsonian, 2003).

20. Forché, *The Country Between Us*, 17, 20.

21. Carolyn Forché, *The Angel of History* (New York: Harper Perennial, 1994); for Benjamin's version of the angel of history see thesis IX of his "Theses on the Philosophy of History" (1940), in *Illuminations*, ed. and trans. Hannah Arendt (New York: Schocken Books, 1969), 257-258.

22. The four excerpts are from Joshua Weiner's review of Scott's *Crossing Borders: Selected Shorter Poems, Boston Review* (February/March 1995): 31; Thom Gunn, "Appetite for Power," *Times Literary Supplement* (1 February 1991): 19; Mary Campbell, "Disaster, or The Scream of Juno's Peacock," *Parnassus* 17:2 & 18:1 (1993): 395; and Robert Hass, "Some Notes on Coming to Jakarta," *AGNI* 31/32 (Winter 1990): 335; and see the collection of six short essays addressing Scott's work in *The Chicago Review* (Winter 1999), 17-50. All further references to Scott's *Coming to Jakarta: A Poem About Terror* (New York: New Directions, 1988) are made within the text.

23. For analyses of Suharto's domination of Indonesia, his brutal 1975 invasion of East Timor, and Jakarta's place in the new global economy, see Benedict Anderson, "Gravel in Jakarta's Shoes," *London Review of Books* (2 November 1995): 2-5; Mark Curtis, "Hawks Over East Timor: Britain Arms Indonesia," *Covert Action Quarterly* 55 (Winter 1995/96): 52-56; and Geraldine Fabrikant, "Family Ties that Bind Growth: Corrupt Leaders in Indonesia Threaten Its Future," *New York Times* (9 April 1996), C1 & 2. The United States was complicit with Suharto's occupation of East Timor and his bloody repression of oppositional groups in Indonesia. In fact, since Suharto's December 1975 invasion of East Timor, in which over 200,000 people—more than 25% of the population—were slaughtered, the U.S. has sold Indonesia over $1.1 billion worth of weapons. The Clinton administration alone sold close to $270 million worth of arms to Suharto; see Jennifer Washburn, "Twist-

ing Arms: The U.S. Weapons Industry Gets Its Way," *The Progressive* (May 1997): 26-27, and Michael Klare, "License to Kill: How the U.S. is Building Up Military-Industrial-Complexes in the Third World," *In These Times* (10 January 1994): 14-19. Suharto was finally forced from power in the spring of 1998. For coverage of his departure see Seth Mydans, "Suharto Steps Down After 32 Years in Power," *New York Times* (21 May 1998), A1 & 8, and any major newspaper during the spring of 1998.

24. Orlando Letelier, the Chilean Ambassador to the United States, was killed by a car bomb in Washington, D.C., in September 1976. Right-wing Cuban expatriates trained by DINA, the Chilean Secret Service, and funded through CIA connections, claimed responsibility for the blast; see Scott's comments in his ground-breaking study, co-authored with Jonathan Marshall, *Cocaine Politics: Drugs, Armies, and the CIA in Central America* (Berkeley: University of California Press, 1991), 30-34.

25. The impulse here is reminiscent of Robert Hass's lament that "There are times/ I wish my ignorance were/ more complete" (from section three of "In Weather," from Hass's *Field Guide* [New Haven, Conn.: Yale University Press, 1973], 61). In fact, Scott later wrote of his "growing self-hatred for carrying around a head full of horrors which most people were less and less willing to hear about"; see his comments in "How I Came to Jakarta," *AGNI* 31/32 (Winter 1990): 300.

26. Edward Sanders, *Investigative Poetry* (San Francisco: City Lights, 1976), 9; like Sanders, Scott is fascinated by Pound and the historiographical possibilities of his *Cantos*—for a cautionary note on Pound see Stephen Hartnett, "The Ideologies and Semiotics of Fascism: Analyzing Pound's *Cantos* 12-15," *boundary 2* 20 (1993): 65-93.

27. See Eyal Press, "The Suharto Lobby," *The Progressive* (May 1997): 19-21; and Anderson, Curtis, Fabrikant, Klare, and Washburn as cited in note 23.

28. Peter Dale Scott, *Listening to the Candle: A Poem on Impulse* (New York: New Directions, 1992), 94; for additional thoughts on this notion of grace see Stephen Hartnett, "Four Meditations on the Search for Grace Amidst Terror," *Text and Performance Quarterly* 19:3 (July 1999): 196-216 and Theresa Carilli, "Verbal Promiscuity or Healing Art? Writing the Creative/Performative Personal Narrative," in *The Future of Performance Studies*, 232-236.

29. Peter Dale Scott, *Minding the Darkness: A Poem for the Year 2000* (New York: New Directions, 2000), the retreat sections are 72-80, 140-148, 221-229, and 244; Scott, "How I Came to Jakarta," 303.

30. Terrence Des Pres, "Poetry and Politics," *TriQuarterly* 65 (Winter 1986): 21; this special issue of *TriQuarterly* is now available as Reginald Gibbons, ed., *The Writer in Our World* (New York: Atlantic Monthly, 1986); for a loving tribute to Des Pres, see Forché's "Ourselves or Nothing," the final poem of *The Country Between Us*, 55-59.

31. Daniel Berrigan, "Rehabilitative Report: We Can Still Laugh," from his *Prison Poems* (Boston: Unicorn Press, 1973), 97; these lines were written while Berrigan was serving a sentence for his activism against the Vietnam War.

32. Carolyn Forché, *Against Forgetting: Twentieth-Century Poetry of Witness* (New York: W. W. Norton, 1993), 40.

33. Sanders, *Investigative Poetry*, 24; Berrigan, "This is About Prayer," *Prison Poems*, 101; for a prose version of these thoughts see Berrigan's conversations with Thich Nhat Hanh, collected as *The Raft is Not the Shore: Conversations Toward a Buddhist-Christian Awareness* (1975; Maryknoll, N.Y.: Orbis, 2001).

Pendleton Poems

1. James Gilligan, "Reflections from A Life Behind Bars: Build Colleges, Not Prisons," *Chronicle of Higher Education* (16 October 1998), B7, 9.

2. Mahdi, quoted in 1994 Indiana Reformatory interview for *Jailbirds*, video documentary by Jon Rutter and Stephen Hartnett.

3. "Trotsky" (*nom de guerre* of Wolfy), "Open Letter from the Pendleton Lockdown," *Prison News Service* 42 (September 1993), 10. This essay was written for one of our classes together in the Indiana Reformatory; Wolfy soon thereafter died of leukemia.

4. Trotsky, *Ibid.*, 10.

5. Kris Wise, "Time to Change," *Kombat* 12 (1995): 27. This poem was performed in one of our classes together in the Indiana Correctional Facility.

6. Jorie Graham, *The Errancy* (Hopewell, N.J.: Ecco Press, 1997), 86.

7. James Stewart, "Conception," in *Extracts from Pelican Bay: An Anthology of Prisoner Poetry, Drawings, and Essays*, ed. Marilla Arguelles (Berkeley: Pantograph, 1995), 14.

8. Daniel Berrigan, "Strip Mining," in *Prison Poems* (Boston: Unicorn, 1973), 110.

9. Hannah Arendt, *On Revolution* (New York: Penguin, 1963), 110.

10. Hannah Arendt, "On Violence," in *Crises of the Republic* (New York: Harcourt, Brace, Jovanovich, 1969), 153.

11. Louis Rodriguez, *Trochemoche* (Willimantic, Conn.: Curbstone, 1998), 79.

12. Tino Villanueva, *Scene from The Movie Giant* (Willimantic, Conn.: Curbstone, 1993), 29.

13. Gilligan, "Reflections from A Life Behind Bars," B9.

14. From Michael Hogan's "Spring," in *Prison Writing in 20th Century America*, ed. H. Bruce Franklin (New York: Penguin, 1998), 246; these lines were written while Hogan was imprisoned in San Quentin. Since his release in 1976, Hogan has cofounded (with Dick Shelton) the Arizona State Prison Writers Workshop and published a number of highly regarded works.

15. James Marquart, "Prison Guards and The Use of Physical Coercion as a Mechanism of Prison Control," *Criminology* 24 (1986): 348, 363.

16. Abraham Lincoln, "The Seventh Joint Debate with Steven Douglas, 15 October 1858," in *The Lincoln-Douglas Debate: The First Complete, Unexpurgated Text,* ed. Harold Holzer (New York: Harper Perennial, 1993), 356.

17. Billy Mason, interview for *Jailbirds*.

18. Lincoln, *Lincoln-Douglas Debate*, 356.

19. Susan Howe, "Encloser," in *The Politics of Poetic Form*, ed. Charles Bernstein (New York: Roof, 1990), 175, 194.

20. Peter Dale Scott and Jonathan Marshall, *Cocaine Politics: Drugs, Armies, and The CIA in Central America* (Berkeley: University of California Press, 1991), viii.

21. Avital Ronell, *Crack Wars: Literature, Addiction, Mania* (Lincoln: University of Nebraska, 1992), 42.

22. Peter Dale Scott, *Listening to the Candle: A Poem on Impulse* (New York: New Directions, 1992), 186.

23. William Bennett, John DiIulio, and John Walters, *Body Count: Moral Poverty and How to Win America's War Against Crime and Drugs* (New York: Simon and Schuster, 1996), 27.

24. Bennett, *Ibid.*, 28, 56, 51.

25. Alice Morse Earle, *Curious Punishments of Bygone Days* (1896; Bedford, Mass.: Applewood, 1995), 143.

26. Sarah Grimké testimony in *American Slavery As It Is: Testimony of A Thousand Witnesses*, ed. Theodore D. Weld (New York: American Anti-Slavery Society, 1839), 23.

27. Paulo Freire, *Pedagogy of the Oppressed*, trans. Myra Bergman Ramos (1970; New York: Continuum, 1994), 62, 71.

28. Anne Greene, "Teaching in Prison is Like Being A Late Night Talk Show Host," *Haight Ashbury Literary Journal* (Winter 1997/98): 12.

"Do Right and Fear Not!": Five Meditations on San Quentin

1. Lionel Ashcroft, "San Quentin Prison: Its Early History and Origins," *Marin County Historical Society* 17 (Spring 1993): 1.

2. James Wilkins, *The Evolution of A State Prison: Historical Narrative of the Ten Years from 1851 to 1861, During the Period when the Care and Employment of Convicts was turned Over to Lessess* (sic), printed in The San Francisco Bulletin, from 13 June 1918 through 10 July 1918, and cited here from a typed manuscript prepared by Clinton Duffy, Warden, California State Prison, San Quentin; held in the archives of The Bancroft Library, University of California, Berkeley, 7.

3. Ashcroft, "San Quentin Prison," 2.

4. From William Wantling, "Sestina for San Quentin," in *Prison Writing in 20th-Century America*, ed. H. Bruce Franklin (New York: Penguin, 1998), 242-43. Unknown in the United States, Wantling enjoyed some international renown for his prison poems; these lines were written while he was serving time in San Quentin from 1958-1964.

5. Umberto Eco, *Foucault's Pendulum*, trans. William Weaver (New York: Harcourt Brace Jovanovich, 1989), 95.

6. Ernst Bloch, *Essays on The Philosophy of Music*, trans. Peter Palmer (1918; Cambridge, UK: Cambridge University Press, 1985), 102, 113, 42.

7. Woody Guthrie, "Do Re Mi," track five on *The Very Best of Woody Guthrie* (Music Collection International, 1992).

8. Shelley Bookspan, *A Germ of Goodness: The California State Prison System, 1851-1944* (Lincoln: University of Nebraska Press, 1991), 2.

9. Malcolm Rohrbough, *Days of Gold: The California Gold Rush and The American Nation* (Berkeley: University of California Press, 1997), 219.

10. Josiah Royce, *California: From the Conquest in 1846 to The Second Vigilance Committee in San Francisco* (New York: Knopf, 1948), 219, 220.

11. Rohrbaugh, *Days of Gold*, 220.

12. Wilkins, *Evolution of a State Prison*, 60.

13. Milo Goss quoted in Rohrbaugh, *Days of Gold*, 159.

14. *Alta* quoted in George Stewart, *Committee of Vigilance: Revolution in San Francisco, 1851* (New York: Houghton Mifflin, 1964), 89.

15. Brannan quoted in Royce, *California*, 323.

16. *Courrier* quoted in Stewart, *Committee of Vigilance*, 94.

17. *Papers of the San Francisco Committee of Vigilance of 1851*, edited by Mary Floyd Williams for *Publications of the Academy of Pacific Coast History, Volume Four* (1919); held in the archives of The Bancroft Library, University of California, Berkeley, 1.

18. *Ibid.*, 1.

19. The banner may be seen in *Papers*, 438.

20. Royce, *California*, 331.

21. Wilkins, *Evolution of a State Prison*, 1.

22. *Papers*, 1, 825-827.

23. *Proclamation!* Poster printed by Governor John McDougal, 20 August 1851; held in the archives of The Bancroft Library, University of California, Berkeley. The original poster is roughly 17" x 24".

24. Ashcroft, "San Quentin Prison," 4.

25. Sailing story from Ward McAfee, "San Quentin: The Forgotten Issue of California's Political History in the 1850s," *Southern California Quarterly* 62 (1990): 238; quotation from Ashcroft, "San Quentin Prison," 6.

26. Wilkins, *Evolution of a State Prison*, 8.

27. Bookspan, *Germ of Goodness*, 5.

28. McAfee, "San Quentin," 237.

29. James Estell, "Speech of General James M. Estell, Delivered in The Hall of Representatives, Sacramento City, California, To a Question of Privilege in Connections with the Vigilance Committee" (1857); held in the archives of The Bancroft Library, University of California, Berkeley, 5.

30. Wilkins, *Evolution of a State Prison*, 22.

31. Ashcroft, "San Quentin Prison," 10.

32. Charles Nordhoff, *California for Travelers and Settlers* (1873; Berkeley: Ten Speed Press, 1974), 100.

33. Wilkins, *Evolution of a State Prison*, 32, 33, 37, 84, 89.

34. McAfee, "San Quentin," 244.

35. The references here, reflecting our class readings, are to Cesare Beccaria, *On Crimes and Punishments and Other Writings*, trans. Richard Davies (1764; Cambridge, UK: Cambridge University Press, 1995), Jeremy Bentham, *The Panopticon Writings* (1787; London: Verso,

1995); Michel Foucault, *Discipline and Punish: The Birth of the Prison*, trans. Alan Sheridan (1975; New York: Random House, 1995); and Peter Linebaugh, *The London Hanged: Crime and Civil Society in the Eighteenth Century* (Cambridge, UK: Cambridge University Press, 1995).

Perhaps Some Grace

1. Mack Jones, "The Black Underclass as Systemic Phenomenon," in *Race, Politics, and Economic Development*, ed. James Jennings (London: Verso, 1992), 59, 53, 59.

2. The Wabash Valley Correctional Facility is in Carlisle, Indiana. When it opened in 1992, it included supermax facilities, hence the protest march depicted here; as of December 2002, the WVCF includes minimum, medium, and maximum security wings. For more information go to the Indiana Department of Corrections Web page: www.in.gov/indcorrection/facil/wabval.html.

3. Herbert Marcuse, *One-Dimensional Man* (Boston: Beacon Press, 1964), 68.

4. Quotation from Julio Rosado, "Political Prisoners in the United States—The Puerto Rican Charade," in *Cages of Steel: The Politics of Imprisonment in the United States*, ed. Ward Churchill (Washington, D.C.: Maisonneuve, 1992): 383; and see the statements by Nelson Ramirez, Filberto Ojeda Rios, Lucy Berrios, and Carmin Valentin, in *Ibid.*, 386-399; on the Fourth World see Ward Churchill, "I am Indigenist: Notes on the Ideology of the Fourth World," in *Struggle for the Land: Indigenous Resistance to Genocide, Ecocide, and Expropriation in Contemporary North America* (Monroe, Maine: Common Courage Press, 1993), 403-451.

5. Eugene Victor Debs, 16 June 1917 "Canton Speech," from *The Debs White Book* (Girard, Kans.: Appeal to Reason, n.d.), 5, 4; on Wilson's wartime repression measures see "An Act to Punish Acts of Interference. . ." (15 June 1917) and "An Act to Amend. . ." (16 April 1918), which together constitute the so called Espionage Acts, from *The Statutes at Large of the United States of America, April 1917–March 1919, volume 50, part two* (Washington, D.C.: Government Printing Office, 1919), 217-231, 531; and see "Chapter 75," the 16 May 1918 amendment regarding sedition to the Espionage Act, in *Statutes of the United States of America, Passed at the Second Session of the Sixty--Fifth Congress, 1917–1918, Part 1: Public Acts and Resolutions* (Washington, D.C.: Government Printing Office, 1918), 553-554.

6. Lincoln comparison from *New York Times*, 14 May 1920, cited in Bernard Brommel, "The Pacifist Speechmaking of Eugene Debs," *Quarterly Journal of Speech* 52 (1966): 153; on Debs running for president see Brommel, 152-154 and Nick Salvatore, *Eugene V. Debs: Citizen and Socialist* (Urbana: University of Illinois Press, 1982).

7. Shaka Shakur, January 1992 letter from the Westville Supermax Prison, reproduced in The Coalition Against Indiana Control Units (CAICU), *Human Rights Violations and Torture on the Rise at the Maximum Control Complex at Westville, IN: Profile of a Supermax* (Chicago: CAICU, 1994), 14.

8. Mike Davis, "Hell Factories in the Field: A Prison-Industrial Complex," *The Nation* (20 February 1995): 229.

9. Paul Wright, "Slaves of the State," *Z Magazine* (July/August 1994): 24; and see Stephen John Hartnett, "Prison Labor, Slavery, and Capitalism in Historical Perspective," *Dark Night Field Notes* 11 (Winter 1998): 25-29.

10. Robert Lilly and Paul Knepper, "The Corrections-Commercial Complex," *Crime and Delinquency* 39:2 (1993): 158; and see Stephen John Hartnett, "Prisons, Profit, Crime, and Social Control: A Hermeneutic of the Production of Violence," in *Race, Class, and Community Identity*, eds. Andrew Light and Meck Nagel (New York: The Humanities Press, 2000), 199-221, and David Shichor, *Punishment for Profit: Private Prisons/Public Concerns* (Thousand Oaks, Calif.: Sage, 1995).

11. Anonymous Campbell's Soup representative quoted in Jon Greenberg, "Building and Maintaining Prisons is a Growth Industry," transcript of report on *All Things Considered* (National Public Radio, 3 August 1994), 15.

12. Stephen Hartnett, "Behavior Modification or Rights Violation?" Indianapolis *Nuvo Newsweekly* (1 June 1994): 10; prison warden quoted from Charles Wright (Superintendent of the Westville Maximum Control Complex), letter to the author, 26 April 1994.

13. See The National Council on Crime and Delinquency, "NCCD Analysis Finds," *Corrections Digest* 25:5 (9 March 1994): 1-4.

14. See American Civil Liberties Union, *Human Rights Violations in the United States* (Washington, D.C.: ACLU, 1993), and CAICU, *Human Rights Violations and Torture on the Rise.*

15. See Jerome Miller, "Interview with Rick Szykowny," *The Humanist* (January/February 1994): 9-19.

16. Debs, "Canton Speech," 26; Debs's "insistent finger" as described by Upton Sinclair in *The Jungle* (1906; New York: New American Library, 1960), 322; and see Ray Ginger, *The Bending Cross: A Bi-*

ography of Eugene Victor Debs (New Brunswick, N.J.: Rutgers University Press, 1949), 357.

17. Wolfgang Haug, *Commodity Aesthetics, Ideology, and Culture* (New York: International General, 1987).

18. From Judee Norton, "Arrival," in *Doing Time: 25 Years of Prison Writing—A PEN American Center Prize Anthology*, ed. Bell Gale Chevigny (New York: Arcade, 1999), 22; Judee wrote these lines in 1990, while doing time in in the Arizona State Prison Complex, Perryville, Arizona.

19. Theodor Adorno and Max Horkheimer, *Dialectic of Enlightenment* (1944; New York: Continuum, 1972), 207.

Emptiness Doesn't Take Notice: Supermax Poems

1. The first half of the title of this poem is a quotation from Jorie Graham, *The Errancy* (Hopewell, N.J.: Ecco Press, 1997), 48; the supermax prison described in "The Tour" is The Maximum Control Complex (MCC) in Westville, Indiana. I have also included additional materials pertaining to the Federal Supermax in Florence, Colorado, and have marked those materials accordingly. For two damning reports on supermaxes see American Civil Liberties Union, *Human Rights Violations in the United States* (Washington, D.C.: ACLU, 1993) and Coalition Against Indiana Control Units, *Human Rights Violations and Torture on the Rise at The Maximum Control Complex at Westville* (Chicago: CAICU, 1994).

2. Dennis Cauchon, "The Alcatraz of the Rockies" and "The 'Baddest of the Bad' Will be Housed Here," *USA Today* (16 November 1994), A6; and see Erica Thompson, "Supermax Prisons: Modern Day Torture in High-Tech Dungeons," *Supplement to Guild Notes* (Fall 1994), 12.

3. William Bennett, John DiIulio, and John Walters, *Body Count: Moral Poverty and How to Win America's War Against Crime and Drugs* (New York: Simon and Schuster, 1996), 27.

4. Graham, *The Errancy*, 36.

5. Dr. Stuart Grassian, quoted in Bruce Porter, "Is Solitary Confinement Driving Charlie Chase Crazy?" *New York Times Magazine* (8 November 1998), 55-56.

6. Porter, *Ibid.*, 58; and see Page Bierma, "Torture Behind Bars," *The Progressive* (July 1994), 21-27.

7. Cauchon, "The Alcatraz of the Rockies," A6.

8. McWhorter quoted in Rick Bragg, "Prison Chief Encouraged Brutality, Witnesses Report," *New York Times* (1 July 1997), A12.

9. McWhorter quoted in Bob Herbert, "Brutality Behind Bars," *New York Times* (7 July 1997), A17.

10. Don Novey, President of The California Correctional Peace Officer's Association (CCPOA), testifying 28 November 1983 before The Joint Committee on Prison Construction and Operations, hearings entitled *California Institution for Men: Present Problems, Cooper Aftermath, Future Needs*; 28 November 1983 (Sacramento, Calif.: n.p., 1983), 61.

11. Pamela Podger, "Lawmakers Demand End to Abuse of Inmates at Prisons," *San Francisco Chronicle* (22 October 1998), A20.

12. Mark Arax and Mark Gladstone, "State Thwarted Brutality Probe at Corcoran, Investigation Says," *Los Angeles Times* (5 July 1998); I'm working here from a version downloaded from the *LAT* Website, and thus do not include page numbers.

13. Arax and Gladstone, "State Thwarted Brutality Probe."

14. *Ibid.*, and see Mark Arax and Mark Gladstone, "Prison Officials to Revise Policy on Deadly Force," *Los Angeles Times* (24 October 1998), A1 & 11.

15. Arax and Gladstone, "State Thwarted Brutality Probe."

16. Facts from California Department of Corrections Website: www.cdc.ca.us/factsht.htm; accessed 12 November 2002.

17. Nils Christie, *Crime Control as Industry: Towards Gulags, Western Style, Second Edition* (London: Routledge, 1994), 112.

18. Mark Arax and Mark Gladstone, "Was Probe of Prison a Whitewash?" *San Francisco Chronicle* (5 July 1998), B6.

19. Podger, "Lawmakers Demand End to Abuse," A16.

20. Connon quoted in Arax and Gladstone, "State Thwarted Brutality Probe."

21. Hayden quoted in Robert Gunnison, "Corcoran Prison Report Doctored, Prober Admits," *San Francisco Chronicle* (31 July 1998), A21.

22. Arax and Gladstone, "State Thwarted Brutality Probe."

23. Corey Weinstein, "Brutality at Corcoran," *California Prison Focus* (Winter 1997): 4; for similar charges regarding brutality at Indiana's MCC Westville see Stephen Hartnett, "Behavior Modification or Rights Violation?" Indianapolis *Nuvo Newsweekly* (1 June 1994), 10.

24. John Rawls, *A Theory of Justice* (Cambridge: Harvard University Press, 1971), 12.

25. Arax and Gladstone, "State Thwarted Brutality Probe."

26. Weinstein, "Brutality at Cororan," 4.

27. David Walker, *Appeal to the Coloured Citizens of the World* (1829; New York: Hill and Wang, 1992), 75.

28. Jean Jacques Rousseau, *Discourse on the Origins and Foundations of Inequality Among Men* (1754; New York: Penguin, 1984), 123.

29. Slaughter figures and Columbus quotation from Howard Zinn, *A People's History of the United States* (New York: Perennial, 1980), 4.

30. Winthrop Jordan, *White Over Black: American Attitudes toward The Negro, 1550-1812* (New York: Norton, 1968), 27.

31. Samuel Cartwright, "Diseases and Peculiarities of the Negro Race," *De Bow's Review* XI (July 1851), reprinted in *The Cause of the South: Selections from De Bow's Review, 1846-1867*, eds. Paul Paskoff and Daniel Wilson (Baton Rouge: Louisiana State University Press, 1982), 34-35.

32. Bennett, *Body Count*, 56.

33. Richard Hernstein and Charles Murray, *The Bell Curve: Intelligence and Class Structure in American Life* (New York: Free Press, 1994), 284.

34. Bennett, *Body Count*, 51.

35. Robert Buchanan, "Report on the Development of James Gordon, Executed at Dumfries, 6th June 1821, for the Murder of John Elliot, a Peddlar Boy," *Transactions of the Phrenological Society* (Edinburgh, UK: John Anderson, 1824), 327-335.

36. BPDS quoted in George Fredrickson, *The Black Image in The White Mind: The Debate on Afro-American Character and Destiny, 1817-1914* (Hanover, N.H.: Wesleyan University Press, 1971), 5.

37. Walker, 53-54; on the history of proslavery rhetoric see Stephen J. Hartnett, *Democratic Dissent & The Cultural Fictions of Antebellum America* (Champaign: University of Illinois Press, 2002), 40-92.

38. Rousseau, *Discourse on the Origins*, 136.

Transcending Schelling's Lament

1. F.W.J. Schelling, *Philosophical Inquiries into the Nature of Human Freedom* (1809: LaSelle, Ill.: Open Court, 1936), 50, 69.

2. *Ibid.*, 79.

3. Thomas Paine, "The Age of Reason" (1794), in *The Thomas Paine Reader* (New York: Penguin, 1987), 400, 403, 421.

4. Schelling, *Philosophical Inquiries*, 29.

5. Georg Lukacs, "On the Romantic Philosophy of Life: Novalis," in *Soul and Form* (1910; Cambridge, Mass.: MIT Press, 1980), 44-45, 50.

6. Schelling, *Philosophical Inquiries,* 95.

7. Ella Fitzgerald, singing Cole Porter's "I Love Paris" (1956 version), on *Ella Fitzgerald Sings the Cole Porter Songbook* (New York: Verve, 1997), disc 2, track 1.

8. Fanny Howe, *One Crossed Out* (Saint Paul, Minn.: Graywolf, 1997), 29.

9. Sigmund Freud, *Group Psychology and the Analysis of the Ego* (1921; New York, Norton, 1989), 91.

10. Aristotle, *The Nicomachean Ethics* (New York: Oxford University Press, 1998), 246.

11. Ann Lauterbach, "Misquotations from Reality," *Diacritics* 26:3 & 4 (Fall/Winter 1996): 143.

12. Etty Ben-Zaken, translator and vocalist, "Mancanica Corelada" (15th Century Sephardic folk song from Sarajevo), performed at Hertz Hall, University of California, Berkeley, 14 October 1998.

13. Freud, *Group Psychology,* 44, 92.

14. Carolyn Forché, *The Country Between Us* (New York: Harper & Row, 1981), 39.

15. Toni Morrison, *Jazz* (New York: Plume, 1992), 96-97.

About the Same as Commercial Fishing

1. "The Dialectic of Perfection and Derangement" is from Fanny Howe, *One Crossed Out* (Saint Paul, Minn.: Graywolf: 1997), 24, which I believe follows from Frederic Jameson's "The Dialectic of Ideology and Utopia" from *The Political Unconscious: Narrative as a Socially Symbolic Act* (Ithaca, N.Y.: Cornell University Press, 1981), 281-299.

2. Lassen Volcanic National Park Web site, "National Park Information," available at www.lassen.volcanic.national-park.com/info.htm.

3. "Headquarters Staff Go to 'Jail' to Raise Nearly $4,000 for United California State Employees Campaign" and "SQ Holds First Employee Recognition Dinner Dance," *Correction News* 10:7 (December 1997/January 1998), 6.

4. Prisoner figure from *CDC Facts, Fourth Quarter 2002,* prepared by The California Department of Corrections; available online at www.cdc.state.ca.us/factsht.htm; dollar figures from Dan Pens, "The California Prison Guards' Union," in *The Celling of America: An Inside Look at the U.S. Prison Industry,* ed. Daniel Burton-Rose (Monroe, Maine: Common Courage, 1998), 134, 135, 138; as discussed in more

detail in "The Gladiators" (pages 79-83 herein;), the CCPOA is The California Correctional Peace Officers Association.

5. Willie Wisely, "Fear and Loathing in California," in Burton-Rose, *Celling of America*, 22; and see Linda Greenhouse, "California's 3-Strikes Law Tested Again," *New York Times* (6 November 2002), A3.

6. Hannah Arendt, *Eichmann in Jerusalem: A Report on the Banality of Evil* (New York: Penguin Books, 1963), 276, 287-288.

7. Lionel Ashcroft, "San Quentin Prison: Its Early History and Origins," *Marin County Historical Society* 17 (Spring 1993): 25.

8. Allen Ginsberg, *Howl and Other Poems* (1956; San Francisco: City Lights Books, 1996), 13.

9. Eugene Victor Debs, *Wall and Bars: Prisons & Prison Life in the "Land of the Free"* (1927; Chicago: Charles Kerr, 2000), 174.

10. Ronald Beattie, *California Prison Population, 1902-1934; Studies in the Administration of Criminal Justice, No. 2* (Sacramento: California Bureau of Public Administration, 1935), 20.

11. Peter Linebaugh, *The London Hanged: Crime and Civil Society in the Eighteenth Century* (Cambridge, UK: Cambridge University Press, 1991), 262.

12. David Rothman, *The Discovery of the Asylum: Social Order and Disorder in the New Republic* (Boston: Little, Brown: 1971), 161.

13. Jean Jacques Rousseau, *Discourse on the Origins and Foundations of Inequality Among Men*, trans. Maurice Cranston (1754; New York: Penguin: 1994), 109.

14. Frank Norris, *The Octopus: A Story of California, The Epic of the Wheat* (1901; New York: Signet, 1964), 388.

15. See *Discover Alcatraz: A Tour of The Rock*, pamphlet published by The Golden Gate National Parks Association, 1996.

16. From Easy (Eric) Waters, "Chronicling Sing Sing Prison," in *Doing Time: 25 Years of Prison Writing—A PEN American Center Prize Anthology*, ed. Bell Gale Chevigny (New York: Arcade, 1999), 76.

17. Carolyn Forché, *The Angel of History* (New York: Harper Perennial, 1994), 15.

18. Carolyn Forché, *The Country Between Us* (New York: Perennial, 1981), 33.

19. Howe, *One Crossed Out*, 4.

20. Charles Burress, "In the Joint, On the Job," *San Francisco Chronicle* (21 September 1998), A17.

21. Peter Dale Scott, *Coming to Jakarta: A Poem About Terror* (New York: New Directions, 1988), 120.

22. Goldman quoted in Burress, "In the Joint," 24.

23. Prisoner figure from California Department of Corrections (CDC) Web site, Pelican Bay State Prison page; available at www.cdc.state.ca.us/facility/instpbsp.htm.

24. Henderson quoted in "Report of February 1996 Investigation of Pelican Bay State Prison," *Pelican Bay Prison Express* 3:3 (April 1996), 2; available from The Pelican Bay Information Project, 2489 Mission St. #28, San Francisco, CA 94110.

25. From CDC Pelican Bay information; see note 23.

26. Cochran quoted in Christian Parenti, *Lockdown America: Police and Prisons in the Age of Crisis* (London: Verso, 1999), 212.

27. Debs, *Walls and Bars*, 135.

28. Shaka, "On Work," essay written in May 1996 for one of our classes in the Indiana Correctional Industrial Facility.

29. E.J. Riley, "Prison: The Labor Camp," essay written in May 1996 for one of our classes in the Indiana Correctional Industrial Facility.

30. James Burkhart, "I Used to Love Work," essay written in May 1996 for one of our classes in the Indiana Correctional Industrial Facility.

31. Paul Wright, "Captive Labor: U.S. Business Goes to Jail," *Covert Action Quarterly* 60 (Spring 1997): 29; and see Stephen Hartnett, "Prison Labor, Slavery, and Capitalism in Historical Perspective," *Dark Night Field Notes* 11 (Winter 1998): 25-29.

32. Burress, "In the Joint," 24.

33. Willie Wisely, "The Bottom Line: California's Prison Industry Authority," in Burton-Rose, *Celling of America*, 140.

34. David Shichor, *Punishment for Profit: Private Prisons/Public Concerns* (Thousand Oaks, Calif.: Sage, 1995), 160; the CCA is The Corrections Corporation of America, now part of a multinational corporation owned by Marriott and Sodexho and dedicated to building prisons, supplying existing prisons with equipment and labor, and sometimes running their own private prisons. For a stunning example of the banality of evil, log on to the CCA's Web site at www.correctionscorp.com.

35. Ron Jacobs, "The New Slave Ships," 5 June 2000; available at www.neravt.com/left/jacobs21.html.

36. Naomi Ayala, *Wild Animals on the Moon* (Willimantic, Conn.: Curbstone, 1998), 36.

Love and Death in California

1. From "Spoon" Jackson's "No Beauty in Cell Bars," in Judith Tannenbaum, *Disguised as a Poem: My Years Teaching Poetry at San*

Quentin (Boston: Northeastern University Press, 2000), 63; and see the information on Jackson at www.spoonjackson.com.

2. Ralph Waldo Emerson, "Love," *Collected Essays* (New York: Houghton and Mifflin, 1865), 137, 142.

3. F.W.J. Schelling, *Philosophical Inquiries into the Nature of Human Freedom* (1809: LaSelle, Ill.: Open Court, 1936), 79.

4. Walt Whitman, "I Cannot be Awake" (1899 fragment), in *The Collected Writings of Walt Whitman*, eds. Gay Wilson Allen and Scully Bradley (New York: New York University Press, 1965), 652.

5. Julia Alvarez, *The Other Side/El Otro Lado* (New York: Plume, 1996), 73.

6. Naomi Ayala, *Wild Animals on the Moon* (Willimantic, Conn.: Curbstone, 1997), 35.

7. Calvin Schrag, *The Self after Postmodernity* (New Haven: Yale University Press, 1997), 143.

8. Immanuel Kant, *Critique of Judgment*, trans. Werner Pluhar (1790; Indianapolis: Hackett, 1994), 129, 105.

9. Carolyn Forché, *The Country Between Us* (New York: Perennial, 1981), 52.

10. Peter Dale Scott, *Listening to the Candle: A Poem on Impulse* (New York: New Directions, 1992), 53.

11. Webster quoted in Thomas Hietala, *Manifest Design: Anxious Aggrandizement in Late Jacksonian America* (Ithaca, N.Y.: Cornell University Press, 1985), 187.

12. See Stephen Vincent Benet, *The Devil and Daniel Webster* (1937; New York: Aeonian Press, 1976).

13. Webster quoted in Rush Welter, *The Mind of America, 1820-1860* (New York: Columbia University Press, 1975), 115.

14. See Kenneth Stampp, *America in 1857: A Nation on the Brink* (New York: Oxford University Press, 1990), 30.

15. "Making a Difference: Oakland's New YWCA at a Glance," pamphlet available at the Oakland YWCA, 1515 Webster Street, Oakland CA, 94612.

16. "Visions of Life: Art Out of Death Row," exhibit of Jay Siripong's art at the Oakland YWCA, 20 January 1998–10 February 1999.

17. R.A. Nelson, "History of Capital Punishment in California," typed ms., no date, 2, held by the Bancroft Library, University of California, Berkeley; Nelson is the retired Associate Warden of San Quentin Prison.

18. Larry Hatfield, "Pope's Plea Can't Halt San Quentin Execution," *San Francisco Examiner* (9 February 1999, evening edition), A1.

19. Peter Dale Scott, *Minding the Darkness: A Poem for the Year 2000* (New York: New Directions, 2000), 20.

20. Karl Marx, "On Capital Punishment" (1853 editorial for *The New York Daily Tribune*), in *Crime and Capitalism*, ed. David Greenberg (Philadelphia: Temple University Press, 1993), 56.

21. Thomas Hobbes, *The Leviathan* (1651; Amherst, N.Y.: Prometheus, 1988), 79.

22. Susan Blaustein, "Witness to Another Execution" (1994), in *The Death Penalty in America*, ed. Hugo Adam Bedau (New York: Oxford University Press, 1997), 395.

23. Quotation from Ron Wikberg, "The Horror Show," in *Life Sentences: Rage and Survival Behind Bars*, eds. Wikberg and Wilbert Rideau (New York: Times Books, 1992), 284. In addition to the horror of his botched electrocution on 4 May 1990, Jesse Tafero was wrongfully executed. The 20 February 1976 double murder of Florida Highway Patrolman Phillip Black and Canadian Constable Donald Irwin, for which Tafero was executed, is now believed to have been committed by Walter Rhodes. Rhodes was the only witness to testify against Tafero; in return for his testimony, Rhodes, who was at the scene of the crime, was allowed to plea bargain for a second-degree murder charge, hence avoiding the death penalty. In essence, Rhodes saved his own life by offering false witness against the innocent Tafero. But Tafero's execution was not only wrongful in the legal sense, it was also politically motivated, as the Judge at Tafero's trial, Daniel Futch, was a recently retired Highway Patrolman who was known throughout the state as "Maximum Dan." His enthusiasm for the death penalty was so great that he kept a miniature electric chair on his desk. The prosecuting attorney in the case, Michael Satz, used his successful conviction of Tafero as a launching point for his candidacy for Broward County District Attorney. Satz won that election and has been in office since then. See "Jesse J. Tafero," in The Grassroots Investigation Project's 26 October 2000 Preliminary Report, *Reasonable Doubts: Is the US Executing Innocent People?*, 27-29 and 68-71. This important document is available from The Quixote Center, P.O. Box 5206, Hyatsville MD 20722; 301-699-0042; www.quixote.org.

24. Immanuel Kant, "Idea for a Universal History from A Cosmopolitan Point of View," in *Kant on History*, ed. Lewis White Beck, (1784; Indianapolis: Bobbs Merrill, 1963), 21-22, 16, 20.

25. Walt Whitman, "Song of the Open Road" (1856 version), in *Leaves of Grass: A Textual Variorum of the Printed Poems, Volume I: Poems, 1855-1856*, eds. Sculley Bradley, Harold Blodgett, Arthur

Golden, and William White (New York: New York University Press, 1980), 229.

Visiting Mario

1. From Kris Kristofferson, "Me and Bobby McGee," on Janis Joplin (with Full Tilt Boogie), *Pearl* (Columbia/Legacy, 1999 reissue)—this version of the song went to Billboard #1 in 1971.

2. From Dar Williams, "After All," track three of *The Green World* (Cooper Station, N.Y.: Razor & Tie Records, 2000).

3. Susan Ferris and Ricardo Sandoval, *The Fight in the Fields: Cesar Chavez and The Farmworkers Movement* (New York: Harcourt Brace, 1997), 82, 117.

4. Woody Guthrie, "Do Re Mi," on *The Limited Collectors Edition of The Very Best of Woody Guthrie* (Hertfordshire, UK: Music Collection International & Folkways, 1992), track five; and check out the gorgeous version of "Do Re Mi" on Nancy Griffith's *Other Voices/Other Rooms* (Los Angeles: Elektra, 1993), track nine.

5. Figures from Criminal Justice Consortium (CJC), *Facts for 1998* (Oakland, Calif.: CJC, 1999), 2, 3; available from the CJC, 1515 Webster Street, Oakland, CA 94612; (510) 836-6065.

6. Excluding the paraphrased dialogue on page 140, italicized passages in this section not attributed to other sources are quotations drawn from: 1) *Mario Rocha, Petitioner, v. C.A. Terhune, Bill Lockyer, Gray Davis, Gil Garcetti, and Does 1 through 10*, 20 October 2000 *Petition for Writ of Habeas Corpus* filed in Superior Court of the State of California for The County of Los Angeles; 2) *Mario Rocha, Petitioner, v. C.A. Terhune, Bill Lockyer, Gray Davis, Gil Garcetti, and Does 1 through 10*, 20 October 2000 *Memorandum of Points and Authorities in Support of Petition for Writ of Habeas Corpus* filed in Superior Court of the State of California for The County of Los Angeles; and 3) *Mario Rocha, Petitioner, v. C.A. Terhune, Bill Lockyer, Gray Davis, Gil Garcetti, and Does 1 through 10*, 20 October 2000 *Declarations in Support of Petition for Writ of Habeas Corpus* filed in Superior Court of the State of California for The County of Los Angeles. To protect witnesses in light of previous threats, Stephen Newman, the remarkable lawyer who filed these documents, has advised me to mask all proper names. Newman may be contacted at Latham & Watkins, Attorneys at Law, 633 West Fifth Street, Suite 400, Los Angeles, CA 90071-2007; (213) 485-1234.

7. Joan Moore, *Homeboys: Gangs, Drugs, and Prison in the Barrios of Los Angeles* (Philadelphia: Temple University Press, 1978), 92, 24.

8. *Salinas Valley State Prison Facts Sheet*, prepared by The California Department of Corrections; available at www.cdc.state.ca.us/facility/instsvsp.htm.

9. Richard Ross, 16 January 2001 letter from death row (prisoner # 50337, P. O. Box 3400, Florence, AZ 85232).

10. Molly Williams, "AuthenTec Sees Wide Use for Fingerprint ID," *Wall Street Journal* (14 December 2000), B12.

11. James Dao, "Pentagon Unveils Plans for a New Crowd-Dispersal Weapon," *New York Times* (2 March 2001), A11.

12. From the fact sheets produced by Stop Prison Rape, available online at www.spr.org.

13. *CDC Facts, Third Quarter 2000*, prepared by The California Department of Corrections; available at www.cdc.state.ca.us/ factsht.htm.

14. BJS, Bureau of Justice Statistics (A), *Incarcerated Parents and Their Children* (Washington, D.C.: Department of Justice, 2000), 1.

15. Eugene Victor Debs, *Wall and Bars: Prisons & Prison Life in the "Land of the Free"* (1927; Chicago: Charles Kerr, 2000), 244.

16. The writing classes described here are run by Sister Janet Harris, one of the nation's true heroes. Harris runs The Inside Out Writers Program, which teaches juvenile prisoners in Los Angeles County how to reclaim their lives through creative writing. Donations, thanks, and inquiries about volunteering should be sent to Inside Out Writers, 23679 Calabasas Road #621, Calabasas CA 91302-1502; InsideOutWriters@aol.com. A similarly important program, this one emphasizing playwriting as a means of coming to consciousness, is Robin Sohnen's Each One Reach One Theatre Program, which may be reached at P.O. Box 1098, Pacifica CA 94044.

17. Bureau of Justice Statistics, *Correctional Populations in the U.S., 1997* (Washington, D.C.: Department of Justice, 2000), 1.

18. William Blum, *Killing Hope: U.S. Military and CIA Interventions since World War II* (Monroe, Maine: Common Courage Press, 1995), 223.

19. Charlie Liteky Diary, entry for 12/26/00; distributed online by CL's friends and available from the author. Thanks to Jason Martin for introducing me to this moving text, cited below as CLD with entry date.

20. Chuck Culhane, "After Almost Twenty Years," in *Doing Time: 25 Years of Prison Writing—A PEN American Center Prize Anthology*, ed. Bell Gale Chevigny (New York: Arcade, 1999), 33-34. Like Mario, Chuck became one of our best poets while in prison; he is now a teacher and activist in New York City.

21. This was Debs's prison address in the Federal Penitentiary in Atlanta; see *Walls and Bars*, 65.

22. *CLD*, 12/24/00.

23. *CLD*, 1/1/01.

24. Calvin Sims, "Argentine Tells of Dumping 'Dirty War' Captives Into Sea," *New York Times* (13 March 1995), A1.

25. Tim Weiner, "Guatemalan Agent of the C.I.A. Linked to Killings of American," *New York Times* (23 March 1995), A1.

26. *CLD*, 1/1/01.

27. *Ibid.*

28. Sister Helen Prejean, *Dead Man Walking*, the quoted verse is a meditative mantra that filters through the version of *Dead Man Walking* performed by The San Francisco Opera, October 2000; music by Jake Heggie, libretto by Terrence McNally. Thanks to Ken Anderson for sharing his libretto.

29. Peter Dale Scott, *Minding the Darkness: A Poem for the Year 2000* (New York: New Directions, 2000), 41.

30. Dar Williams, "I Had no Right," track nine of *The Green World*.

About the Author

Stephen John Hartnett is Assistant Professor of Speech Communication at The University of Illinois, where he is a member of the American Studies Working Group, an advisor to The Center for Democracy in a Multiracial Society, and one of the university's 2003/2004 Helen Corley Petit Scholars. He is the author of *Democratic Dissent & The Cultural Fictions of Antebellum America*, which won the National Communication Association's 2002 Winans and Wichelns Memorial Award for Distinguished Scholarship in Rhetoric and Public Address, and co-author, with the late Robert James Branham, of *Sweet Freedom's Song: "My Country 'Tis of Thee" and Democracy in America*. His work as a rhetorical scholar of American history has appeared in *American Studies, Argumentation and Advocacy, Boundary 2, Cultural Critique, Philosophy and Rhetoric, The Quarterly Journal of Speech, A Rhetorical History of the Unites States* (volumes I and III, forthcoming), and *Text and Performance Quarterly*. His work as an activist, poet, and critic of the prison-industrial-complex has appeared in *Broken Chains, The Journal of Contemporary Criminal Justice, Dark Night Field Notes, The Future of Performance Studies, The Journal of Applied Communication Research, Left Curve, LIP,* and *The Radical Philosophy Review*. Prior to entering the academy, Hartnett had a successful musical career, including writing, performing, and co-producing three critically acclaimed recordings with The Icemakers of the Revolution, a Midwestern rock-n-roll band. From 1990-1996 he taught college in Indiana prisons; from 1996-1999 he taught college in California's San Quentin Prison. He is currently working on *The Waiting Room*, an interactive art installation organized around community conversations about the death penalty, and *Executing Democracy: Arguing About Capital Punishment in America, 1683-1845*. He is married to Brett Kaplan and lives in Champaign, Illinois.